How big an '80s movie freak are you? If you know which character in which movie said these lines, you're definitely stuck in the decade of Day-Glo . . .

- "That's classified information. I could tell you, but then I'd have to kill you."

- "I'm gonna let you in on a little secret, Ray. Kmart sucks."

- "I can't believe my grandmother actually felt me up!"

- "Joe, she's written sixty-five songs about you and they're all about pain."

Peter T. Fornatale spent the entire '80s memorizing lyrics to Bruce Springsteen songs and movie quotes from the film *Tron*. He has written comedy for radio, liner notes, and copy for Elvis Presley trading cards. Frank R. Scatoni spent his free time in the '80s watching *Sixteen Candles* and Molly Ringwald's first flick, *Tempest*. He is a former magazine writer. Both authors currently work at New York publishing houses. Together they are the authors of *Who Can It Be Now? The Lyrics Game That Takes You Back to the '80s . . . One Line at a Time*.

Also by the authors

*Who Can It Be Now? The Lyrics Game That Takes You Back
to the '80s . . . One Line at a Time*

say anything

the
movie quote game
that takes you back to
the '80s
one line at a time

Peter T. Fornatale
and Frank R. Scatoni

a plume book

PLUME
Published by the Penguin Group
Penguin Putnam Inc., 375 Hudson Street, New York, New York 10014, U.S.A.
Penguin Books Ltd, 27 Wrights Lane, London W8 5TZ, England
Penguin Books Australia Ltd, Ringwood, Victoria, Australia
Penguin Books Canada Ltd, 10 Alcorn Avenue, Toronto, Ontario, Canada M4V 3B2
Penguin Books (N.Z.) Ltd, 182–190 Wairau Road, Auckland 10, New Zealand

Penguin Books Ltd, Registered Offices:
Harmondsworth, Middlesex, England

First published by Plume,
a member of Penguin Putnam Inc.

First Printing, November, 1999
10 9 8 7 6 5 4 3 2 1

Copyright © Peter T. Fornatale and Frank R. Scatoni, 1999
All rights reserved.
All photos courtesy of Photofest.

  REGISTERED TRADEMARK—MARCA REGISTRADA

LIBRARY OF CONGRESS CATALOGING-IN-PUBLICATION DATA:
Fornatale, Peter.
Say anything : the movie quote game that takes you back to the '80s one line at a time /
Peter T. Fornatale and Frank R. Scatoni.
p.   cm.
ISBN 0-452-28147-4
1. Motion pictures Quotations, maxims, etc.   2. Motion pictures Miscellanea.
I. Scatoni, Frank R.   II. Title.
PN1994.9.F675   1999
791.43—dc21   99-34509
                                                                          CIP

Printed in the United States of America
Set in Officina Sans Book and Janson Text
Designed by Blue Farm Bookworks

BOOKS ARE AVAILABLE AT QUANTITY DISCOUNTS WHEN USED TO PROMOTE PRODUCTS OR SERVICES. FOR INFORMATION PLEASE WRITE TO PREMIUM MARKETING DIVISION, PENGUIN PUTNAM INC., 375 HUDSON STREET, NEW YORK, NEW YORK 10014.

To Big John Studd,
Junkyard Dog,
André "the Giant"
Rousimoff,
Kerry Von Erich, and
Owen Hart.

May you all vie for the
Intercontinental championship
in the great squared circle
in the sky.

And to the great Señor Wences:
S'all right?
S'all right!

Acknowledgments

Thanks to our agent, Todd Keithley of Jane Dystel Literary Management, who once again was an incredible help during every stage of this process. To our editor, Jennifer Moore, for her invaluable guidance and support, and all the other folks at Plume who backed *Say Anything*—thank you.

We'd also like to thank Jennifer Thornton for all her suggestions that made this book so much better. And to Susan Van Metre, committed X-Filer, whose knowledge of *Ghostbusters* helped us flesh out portions of this book.

Our team of researchers, who sat through the likes of *Meatballs III* and *She-Devil*, also deserve kudos. They include Matt Blankman, Jeff Colchamiro, Marian Courtney, Scott Cupolo, Colette Ellis, Mark Fornatale, Steven Fornatale, Barbara Hauley, Justin Heimberg, Rachel Kahan, Robert Kempe, Bob Mecoy, Lindsay Mergens, Lucia Quartararo, Brant Rumble, Kim Scatoni, Lisa Scatoni, and Jon Tannen.

Thanks to the world's greatest web site, IMDB (Internet Movie Database); the coolest stock house in town, Photofest; and all the actors, writers, directors, and producers who appear in the pages of this book.

Finally, many thanks to both of our families. Without them, none of this would be possible. *That's the fact, Jack!*

Introduction

1939: "Frankly, my dear, I don't give a damn."

1942: "Here's looking at you, kid."

1954: "I could've been a contender."

1969: "I'm walkin' here."

1972: "I'm gonna make him an offer he can't refuse."

1984: "I can't believe I gave my panties to a geek."*

Okay, so maybe the '80s weren't the proudest decade in cinematic history, but for us they were the most memorable. In *Say Anything* we've given you more than five hundred quotes from the best and worst of the decade to test your mettle and assess your '80s movie acumen. Your mission: Name the movie the quote is from and the character who said it. You think it's easy? Wait until you start playing. As for the '80s movie quote above, it was spoken by Samantha—played by '80s teen-movie supernova Molly Ringwald—in *Sixteen Candles*. But can you tell us who said the following immortal lines?

"I am your father."

"Heeeeeere's Johnnie!"

"You'll get nothing and like it."

If you said Darth Vader from *The Empire Strikes Back*, Jack Torrance from *The Shining*, and Judge Smails from *Caddyshack*, then *Say Anything* is the book for you. If you don't know who Darth Vader is, check out the *Matlock* marathon coming soon to a superstation near you.

*Incidentally, these other lines are from *Gone With the Wind*, *Casablanca*, *On the Waterfront*, *Midnight Cowboy*, and *The Godfather*. If you didn't recognize a single one of these, we suggest you seriously reconsider your life's calling—your obvious hermetic personality is perfect for the isolationist practices of monasteries and federal maximum security prisons. Good luck!

"Phone home."

Okay, we decided to let you off easy on this one. If you didn't get this, do us all a favor and go back to the bookstore, get your money refunded, and put it toward Oprah's book of the month. We hear it's a beautiful, well-told saga of a woman facing adversity and learning life's most important lesson. Oh wait, that was last month.

Steven Spielberg's ***E.T. The Extra-Terrestrial*** is one of the highest-grossing pictures of all time. It also marked the on-screen debut of the cult-game phenomenon Dungeons & Dragons. As a result of the exposure, Gary Gygax's already popular role-playing game exploded. They even made a Saturday morning cartoon show of D & D with Ralph Malph (Donny Most) voicing one of the main characters, Eric "the Cavalier." If you haven't figured it out by now, this quote was spoken by the short, wrinkle-faced alien, **E.T.**

"People on 'ludes should not drive."

As a matter of fact, **Jeff Spicoli** (Sean Penn) in *Fast Times at Ridgemont High* probably shouldn't have done a lot of things. His drugged-out surfer boy antics inspired a whole generation of wannabes who mangled the English language (*gnarly!*) and tried to order pizza in class. *Fast Times* served as a launching pad for many actors and actresses who went on to make it big: Penn, Nicolas Cage, Eric Stoltz, Jennifer Jason Leigh, Judge Reinhold, Anthony Edwards, Phoebe Cates, and Forest Whitaker. (Even writer Cameron Crowe went on to garner an Oscar nomination for penning *Jerry Maguire*.) Of course, not all of the cast members became household names. If you're wondering where the guy who played Mike Damone (Robert Romanus) is now, so are we.

"Aloha, Mr. Hand."

Deities of the '80s—Tom Cruise

Not every actor who sports Ray Bans and dances around the house wearing his underwear and a white oxford hits the big time. But Mr. Cruise certainly did. While Bob Seger—whose song "Old Time Rock & Roll" provided the soundtrack for Cruise's little striptease—went on to peddle Ford trucks with "Like a Rock," Cruise went on to superstardom in the '90s, commanding one of the highest salaries in all of Hollywood. His marriage to Nicole Kidman in 1990 frustrated men and women and Mimi Rogers alike, but Tom and Nicole have proven to be the perfect Hollywood couple (or at least our legal advisors tell us so). And while Mimi recaptured some of her past celebrity as Mrs. Kensington in 1997's *Austin Powers* and in her role as Agent Diana Fowley in television's *The X-Files*, the early '90s must have been a really tough time for her. While Tom was busy starring in *Days of Thunder* with his wife-to-be, Mimi was preparing for her *Playboy* pictorial and producing *Designated Hitter*, a game show for ESPN.

So you think you know Tom Cruise movies? Well, what character said the following lines and what movies are they from? Don't worry, there's nothing from *Legend*.

1. "That's classified information. I could tell you, but then I'd have to kill you."
2. "I'm gonna let you in on a little secret, Ray. Kmart sucks."
3. "I think maybe the money's what's throwing you off here today."
4. "It seems to me that if there were any logic to our language, *trust* would be a four-letter word."
5. "I make things with juice and froth, the pink squirrel, the three-toed sloth."
6. "People say that if you don't love America, then get the hell out. Well, I love America."
7. "Ain't nobody gonna call the fuzz in this neighborhood 'cause they know better."

1. **Pete "Maverick" Mitchell** in *Top Gun*
2. **Charlie Babbitt** in *Rain Man*
3. **Vincent Lauria** in *The Color of Money*
4. **Joel Goodson** in *Risky Business*
5. **Brian Flanagan** in *Cocktail*
6. **Ron Kovic** in *Born on the Fourth of July*
7. **Steve Randle** in *The Outsiders*

"Do you ever get the feeling that there's something going on that we don't know about?"

Spoken by Kevin Bacon, the Six Degree Man himself (as **Timothy Fenwick Jr.**), this question is just one of the many great lines in Barry Levinson's classic *Diner.* Our favorite scene in the movie is the one where Eddie (Steve Guttenberg) makes his fiancée take an SAT-level test about football and the history of the Baltimore Colts before he'll agree to walk down the aisle. Not such a bad idea when you think about it.

Like *American Graffiti* before it, *Diner* was a coming-of-age movie whose stable of young actors were unknown at the time but went on to stardom—or at least the central role in a handful of *Police Academy* movies.

"You can't compare Mathis to Sinatra. There's no way. They're in totally different leagues."

How did TriStar Pictures convince '80s moviegoers to see a movie about some Indian guy and an escaped robot? They got El DeBarge to perform the movie's theme song, of course. Who can forget "Who's Johnny" (from *Short Circuit*) and the maddening adventures of the irrepressible No. Five? Come on, we know you've seen both *Short Circuit* and *Short Circuit II*, and we know that "Who's Johnny" is one of your favorite songs. So we invite you to sing along with us: " 'Who's Johnny?' she said, and smiled in her special way . . ." Okay, enough of that. But really, almost every major '80s movie had a hit single released from its soundtrack. We've listed a few movie quotes below. Can you tell us the character, the movie, and the name of that movie's most popular single and the artist who performed it?

1. "Life moves pretty fast. If you don't stop and look around once in a while, you could miss it."

2. "I'm going to Hawaii. I'm going to Hawaii. . . . I'm not going to Hawaii!"

3. "So what's a dancer doing working as a welder?"

4. "A radio shrink? They're only good for people with problems that fit between the commercials."

5. "I find it hard to imagine your wife sleeping with you."

6. "Sometimes you just gotta say, 'What the heck.' "

7. "How about a nice greasy pork sandwich served in a dirty ashtray?"

8. "Break his heart, I'll break your face."

1. **Ferris Bueller** (Matthew Broderick) in ***Ferris Bueller's Day Off*** ("Oh Yeah" by Yello)

2. **Monty Capuletti** (Rodney Dangerfield) in ***Easy Money*** ("Easy Money" by Billy Joel)

3. **Nick Hurley** (Michael Nouri) in ***Flashdance*** ("Maniac" by Michael Sembello or "Flashdance . . . What a Feeling" by Irene Cara)

4. **Jonathan Switcher** (Andrew McCarthy) in ***Mannequin*** ("Nothing's Gonna Stop Us Now" by Starship)

5. **Buddy** (Charles Grodin) in ***The Woman in Red*** ("I Just Called to Say I Love You" by Stevie Wonder)

6. **Joel's Father** (Nicholas Pryor) in ***Risky Business*** ("Old Time Rock & Roll" by Bob Seger)

7. **Chet** (Bill Paxton) in ***Weird Science*** ("Weird Science" by Oingo Boingo)

8. **Watts** (Mary Stuart Masterson) in ***Some Kind of Wonderful*** ("I Go Crazy" by Flesh for Lulu)

"No more yankie my wankie. The Donger
need food."

If you need proof that the Golden Age of the teen movie occurred long before the age of political correctness, look no further than John Hughes's directorial debut, **Sixteen Candles.** Starring Molly Ringwald as Samantha and Anthony Michael Hall as The Geek/Farmer Ted, *Sixteen Candles* became the prototypical '80s teen movie. This line is spoken by Gedde Watanabe, who plays Chinese exchange student **Long Duk Dong**—perhaps the most over-the-top Asian stereotype since Mickey Rooney's Mr. Yunioshi in *Breakfast at Tiffany's.*

"Go ahead, make my day."

Everybody from the '80s, with the possible exception of Ronald Reagan (who once aped it), remembers that this line is said by Clint Eastwood as **Dirty Harry Callahan.** But do you remember that it's from the fourth Dirty Harry movie, ***Sudden Impact***? Like all four Dirty Harry sequels, the movie itself was quite forgettable—although the fifth and final one, *The Dead Pool,* is worth watching just to see Liam Neeson, Jim Carrey, and Guns n' Roses in the supporting cast.

Clint has received much deserved respect from fans and critics alike for his acting and directorial work in great films like *The Outlaw Josey Wales* and *Unforgiven*. It becomes easy to forget that this is the same guy who milked the Dirty Harry cow five times and twice costarred with an orangutan.

Tearjerkers

All right, we admit it—even we wept during *Terms of Endearment*. It doesn't get any more depressing than a young mother of three dying of cancer. So for all you depressed souls out there who are gluttons for punishment, take out your boxes of Kleenex and enjoy these lines from the teariest tearjerkers of the decade.

1. "What's yodeling got to do with it?"
2. "I was just curious: Did you have any reaction at all when I said I loved you?"
3. "It's really important to try to hurt me, isn't it?"
4. "I don't know how to fight. All I know how to do is stay alive."
5. "I'd rather have thirty minutes of wonderful than a lifetime of nothing special."

1. **C C Bloom** (Bette Midler) in *Beaches*
2. **Aurora Greenway** (Shirley MacLaine) in *Terms of Endearment*
3. **Beth Jerrod** (Mary Tyler Moore) in *Ordinary People*
4. **Young Celie** (Desreta Jackson) in *The Color Purple*
5. **Shelby** (Julia Roberts) in *Steel Magnolias*

"Twice I took the name of the Lord in vain, once I slept with the brother of my fiancé, and once I bounced a check at the liquor store, but that was really an accident."

"When the moon hits your eye, like a big-a pizza pie—that's amore!"
(For more on Dean Martin, turn to page 118.)

Moonstruck remains one of the most beloved romantic comedies from the '80s—largely the result of the on-screen chemistry between Nicolas Cage (playing the one-handed Ronny Cammareri) and inaugural member of the reconstructive surgery hall of fame, Cher (as **Loretta Castorini**). Let's all take a moment to be thankful that the role didn't end up going to Sally Field as was originally planned. Can you imagine Gidget in a faux Italian accent slapping Cage and saying, "Snap out of it!"?

It's All Ball Bearings Nowadays: Lines from *Fletch*

One of the more eminently quotable movies of the decade, *Fletch*—adapted from the Gregory McDonald novel of the same name—solidified Chevy Chase's career as a successful comedic actor (as opposed to an unsuccessful late-night talk-show host). Whether he was Irwin M. Fletcher, Ted Nugent, Arnold Babar, Mr. Poon, Igor Stravinsky, Gordon Liddy, Don Corleone, Harry S. Truman, or a star Lakers forward, Fletch entertained with his quick wit ("You using the whole fist, Doc?") and bizarre humor ("Just bring me a glass of hot fat and the head of Alfredo Garcia while you're there."*). Below are five lines from *Fletch*. Most, but not all, were said by Fletch himself. The trick here is to name the character Fletch was impersonating when he said the line.

1. "Does this proposition entail me dressing up as Little Bo Peep?"
2. "Somebody's buckin' for a promotion—probably that pederast Hanrahan."
3. "Moe Green is out of the Tropicana now. My sons Mike and Fredo are taking over."
4. "What can I say about Fletch? He boxes out for us."
5. "Aw, c'mon guys, it's so simple. Maybe you need a refresher course. It's all ball bearings nowadays."

*An allusion to the 1974 Sam Peckinpah film *Bring Me the Head of Alfredo Garcia* and not a reference to mediocre '80s middle infielders Alfredo Griffin (Toronto Blue Jays) and Kiko Garcia (Baltimore Orioles).

1. **Ted Nugent** (Chevy Chase)
2. **Mr. Poon** (Chevy Chase)
3. **Don Corleone** (Chevy Chase)
4. **Kareem Abdul-Jabbar** (as himself)
5. **Gordon Liddy** (Chevy Chase)

"Six-five—with the afro, six-nine."

"They're here."

What do you think is more scary: The fact that several cast members from the ***Poltergeist*** trilogy died mysterious deaths? Or the fact that *Coach*, starring *Poltergeist* dad Craig T. Nelson, was on week in and week out for more than ten years? We'll let you decide about that. Meanwhile, here's our memento mori for the *Poltergeist* cast and crew:

• Heather O'Rourke **(Carol Anne Freeling),** the sweet, adorable actress who uttered that famous line, died tragically at the age of twelve of a congenital intestinal disorder in 1988.

• Dominique Dunne (Dana Freeling), daughter of Dominick and sister of Griffin, was strangled to death by her boyfriend shortly after the release of the first film in 1982.

• Julian Beck (Kane) died of stomach cancer before the release of *Poltergeist II* in 1985.

• Will Sampson (Taylor) died from complications during surgery in 1987.

Deities of the '80s—Kathleen Turner

What's the most impressive thing about Kathleen Turner? Her acting? Her looks? Her amazing voice?

All those are acceptable answers, but we're more impressed with her ability to capture the imagination of '80s musicians. First, the late, great Falco was inspired enough by Ms. Turner to write his club hit "The Kiss of Kathleen Turner." Maybe it wasn't as popular as "Der Kommissar" or "Rock Me Amadeus," but it should have been. And then, Billy Ocean recruited her to be in his video for "When the Going Gets Tough, the Tough Get Going." Even the most hard-hearted critic would have to admire a woman who appeals to Austrian technopop darling and Caribbean fashion plate alike. Everyone remembers Turner as the voice of the second-hottest cartoon character in history (after Olive Oyl of course), Jessica Rabbit. But few remember that her electronically altered voice also appeared in the somewhat less sexy movie *GoBots: Battle of the Rock Lords.*

1. "You're not too smart, are you? I like that in a man."
2. "*The Complete Poems of John Lillison,* England's greatest one-armed poet."
3. "It was Grogan: the filthiest, dirtiest, dumbest excuse for a man west of the Missouri River."
4. "I'm a hooker. You're a trick. Why ruin a perfect relationship?"
5. "My husband was pretty f**kin' smart."
6. "You bought an Edsel!"
7. "There's something so muffled about the way you experience things."
8. "I'm not bad, I'm just drawn that way."
9. "Have you ever made angry love?"
10. "Don't be ridiculous. Jack would never die without telling me."

1. **Matty Walker** in *Body Heat*
2. **Dolores Benedict** in *The Man with Two Brains*
3. **Joan Wilder** in *Romancing the Stone*
4. **Joanna Crane/China Blue** in *Crimes of Passion*
5. **Irene Walker** in *Prizzi's Honor*
6. **Peggy Sue Bodell** in *Peggy Sue Got Married*
7. **Sarah Leary** in *The Accidental Tourist*
8. **Jessica Rabbit** in *Who Framed Roger Rabbit*
9. **Barbara Rose** in *The War of the Roses*
10. **Joan Wilder** in *The Jewel of the Nile*

"I need the kiss of Kathleen Turner right now. Smack! In the middle."— Falco

"I know I'm only a freshman, but what do you say you and I have dinner tonight? We can talk about Joyce. She's my favorite writer."

Back to School, like its star Rodney Dangerfield, gets no respect. But that doesn't stop it from being one of the funniest movies of the '80s. The film features great comic performances from Sally Kellerman, Sam Kinison, Burt Young,* and Dangerfield as **Thornton Melon,** the successful clothier who goes back to get a college degree to help out his son. But the funniest moment in the movie belongs to a writer, not an actor. Kurt Vonnegut—doing a walk-on as himself—is hired by Melon to write a paper about . . . Kurt Vonnegut. It gets a failing grade. The professor's (Sally Kellerman) comment: "I'll tell you something else. Whoever did write it doesn't know the first thing about Kurt Vonnegut."

[*In case you're wondering, Burt's Italian restaurant in the Bronx, Il Boschetto, is fantastic! We suggest the chicken saltimbocca.]

"Now that's what I call marine biology."

Well, we've given you the luxury of theme sections to give you clues to the movies and the characters. Now try working without a net.

1. "Like, he's got the bod, but his brains are bad news."
2. "Do you like sushi like I like sushi?"
3. "It's better to be a live dog than a dead lion."
4. "Sidney, don't say a f**king thing or I'll bury this phone in your head!"
5. "This dream is short, but this dream is happy."
6. "They used to call me Crazy Joe. Well, now they can call me Batman!"
7. "I might as well pin a hundred-dollar bill to my butt and scream, 'Victim here! Victim here!'"
8. "Have you ever heard the expression 'kissed by a muse'? Well, that's what I am. I'm a muse."
9. "Why, Ted Striker's got more guts in his little finger than most of us have in our large intestine, including the colon!"
10. "I don't know what to do with you. You're a nice guy."
11. "I hate this freakin' place. I detest it like a sickness."
12. "It's good to be the king."
13. "Did anyone ever tell you that you have the face of a Botticelli and the body of a Degas?"
14. "No money, no job, no rent. Hey, I'm back to normal."
15. "Ethel Thayer. Sounds like I have a lisp, doesn't it?"
16. "I'm pregnant. Can you pass the turnips?"
17. "You're an alien and I'm from the Valley."
18. "How could a righteous babe like you be lonely?"
19. "We got a secret weapon. God is our copilot."

1. **Julie** (Deborah Foreman) in *Valley Girl*
2. **Bruce** (Johnny Yune) in *They Call Me Bruce?*
3. **Charles Driggs** (Jeff Daniels) in *Something Wild*
4. **Jimmy Serrano** (Dennis Farina) in *Midnight Run*
5. **Leni Lamaison/Marta/Spider Woman** (Sonia Braga) in *Kiss of the Spider Woman*
6. **Joe Clark** (Morgan Freeman) in *Lean on Me*
7. **Terry Doolittle** (Whoopi Goldberg) in *Jumpin' Jack Flash*
8. **Kira** (Olivia Newton-John) in *Xanadu*
9. **McCroskey** (Lloyd Bridges) in *Airplane II: The Sequel*
10. **Isabelle "Izzy" Grossman** (Amy Irving) in *Crossing Delancey*
11. **Pino** (John Turturro) in *Do the Right Thing*
12. **Louis XVI** (Mel Brooks) in *History of the World Part I*
13. **Jack Jericho** (Robert Downey Jr.) in *The Pick-up Artist*
14. **Henry Chinaski** (Mickey Rourke) in *Barfly*
15. **Norman Thayer Jr.** (Henry Fonda) in *On Golden Pond*
16. **Darcy** (Molly Ringwald) in *For Keeps*
17. **Valerie Dale** (Geena Davis) in *Earth Girls Are Easy*
18. **Daryl** (Anthony Rapp) in *Adventures in Babysitting*
19. **Fenderbaum** (Sammy Davis Jr.) in *The Cannonball Run*

"Greed, for lack of a better word,
is good."

Another easy one, this line was said by **Gordon Gekko** (Michael Douglas, who won an Oscar for this role) to Bud Fox (a prewhoremonger Charlie Sheen) in Oliver Stone's *Wall Street*.

While we're not big fans of Stone's (we like having popcorn at the movies, not Dramamine), we'll give him this one. *Wall Street* did effectively define a brief, troubled moment of time in the late '80s—when insider trading threatened our nation's economy and Daryl Hannah got leading roles.

Make Love Not War

What movie is "Shall we play a game" from?

If you guessed *WarGames*, then you are one hundred percent correct. The line, of course, was spoken by the computer, Joshua, to David Lightman (Matthew Broderick), the computer hacker who nearly started World War III. Luckily, the fate of the Western world was left in the hands of '80s movies icons Broderick and Ally Sheedy, who had to convince Joshua that they only wanted to play tic-tac-toe and not to start a global thermonuclear war. The lines listed below are quotes from actual war movies. You know, the kind where people get shot, villages get blown up, and Vietnamese prostitutes seduce strapping young American men by saying, "Me so horny. Me love you long time." Now that's what war is all about. So for you war junkies out there, here are a few war movies to keep you busy until *Saving Private Ryan II* comes to a theater near you.

1. "If you flunk out and die in Vietnam, that's the end of our friendship."
2. "Nothing's forgiven. Nothing."
3. "Shoot straight, you bastards. Don't make a mess of it!"
4. "A colored soldier can stop a bullet as good as a white."
5. "I've drank more beer, pissed more blood, and banged more quiff than all you numb-nuts put together."
6. "You on my frequency?"
7. "Somebody once wrote, 'Hell is the impossibility of reason.' That's what this place feels like. Hell."
8. "Cockatoos. Sunset. They'll lead you straight to it."
9. "Tell me. What's the difference between us and them?"
10. "Didn't mommy and daddy show you enough attention when you were a child?"

1. **Scott** (Kiefer Sutherland) in *1969*
2. **Dith Pran** (Haing S. Ngor) in *The Killing Fields*
3. **Lieutenant Harry Morant** (Edward Woodward) in *Breaker Morant*
4. **Trip** (Denzel Washington) in *Glory*
5. **Gunnery Sergeant Tom Highway** (Clint Eastwood) in *Heartbreak Ridge*
6. **Captain Hill** (Dale Dye) in *Casualties of War*
7. **Chris Taylor** (Charlie Sheen) in *Platoon*
8. **Archy** (Mark Lee) in *Gallipoli*
9. **Matt** (Charlie Sheen) in *Red Dawn*
10. **Gunnery Sergeant Hartman** (Lee Ermey) in *Full Metal Jacket*

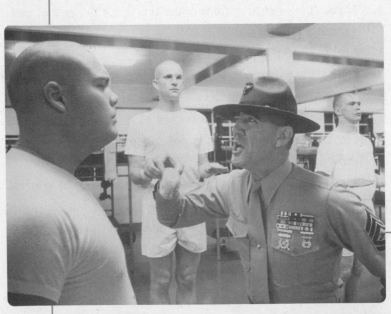

"You can give your heart to Jesus, but your ass belongs to the corps."

"Our pizza—it's tradition. You don't monkey with tradition!"

Long before **Mystic Pizza** the movie there was Mystic Pizza the restaurant. Founded in 1973, Mystic Pizza has been serving the bustling shipbuilding community of Mystic, Connecticut, ever since their first crisp, cheesy pie came out of the oven. In the late '80s, Amy Holden Jones used the restaurant as the inspiration to tell the coming-of-age stories of three young women—**Daisy,** Kat, and Jojo—who work at the pizzeria. Julia Roberts (who played Daisy) used *Mystic Pizza* to launch a successful movie career. Mystic Pizza used *Mystic Pizza* to launch a successful line of frozen pies. Look for them at a supermarket near you.

Mystic Pizza Ingredients

Crust: *flour, water, corn oil, yeast, sugar, salt, baking powder*
Toppings: *low-moisture part-skim mozzarella, cheddar, water, tomato paste, sugar, granulated garlic, spices, salt, Romano cheese (made from cow's milk)*

"I think that the problem may have been that there was a Stonehenge monument on the stage that was in danger of being crushed by a dwarf."

This Is Spinal Tap is the funniest documentary—"rockumentary, if you will"—of all time. Directed by Rob Reiner (Meathead! Can you believe it?) and starring Michael McKean (Lenny of Lenny and Squiggy), Christopher Guest, Harry Shearer, and Tony Hendra, *This Is Spinal Tap* became an instant cult hit. The hilarious antics of **David St. Hubbins,** Nigel Tufnel, Derek Smalls, and their manager, Ian Faith, added to the spoof documentary genre in the same tradition as Eric Idle's *The Rutles* and Albert Brooks's *Real Life*. And if you want our pick for the funniest scene of the movie, it's when the band closes the partition on the limo driver (played by Bruno Kirby) just as he breaks into his "Are you reading *Yes I Can* by Sammy Davis Jr.?" spiel. "You know what that book should be called? 'Yes I Can as Long as Frank Sinatra Says It's Okay.' "

"Do you have any artificial plates or limbs?"

This Is Spinal Tap Matching Game

Can you match the cameos with their character names?

a. Mime Waiter

b. Lieutenant Hookstratten

1. **Fran Drescher**   c. Polly Deutsch

2. **Billy Crystal**   d. Bobbi Flekman

3. **Bruno Kirby**   e. Morty the Mime

4. **Paul Shaffer**   f. Terry Ladd

5. **Dana Carvey**   g. Tommy Pischedda

6. **Ed Begley Jr.**   h. Artie Fufkin

7. **Howard Hesseman**   i. John "Stumpy" Pepys

8. **Anjelica Huston**

9. **Fred Willard**

1. **d**

2. **e**

3. **g**

4. **h**

5. **a**

6. **i**

7. **f**

8. **c**

9. **b**

Deities of the '80s—Eddie Murphy

Sure, *48 Hrs.* and *Beverly Hills Cop* are considered Eddie Murphy's crowning '80s achievements. But *Coming to America* is by far the funniest (and most unheralded) Murphy movie of all time. In it, Murphy plays about a dozen characters—from a "Soul Glo"–dripping gospel singer to a crotchety old white man—with each one funnier than the last. The best scenes of the movie come in the neighborhood barbershop where Murphy and Arsenio Hall (as aging barbers) argue about everything from Martin Luther King Jr. ("You ain't never seen Dr. Martin Luther King with no messy Jheri curl on his head") to boxing ("Every time I start talkin' 'bout boxing a white man got to pull Rocky Marciano out their ass"). And believe it or not, the usually annoying Arsenio Hall ("ooh-ooh-ooh") is actually brilliant as Murphy's attendant and various sidekicks throughout the movie. In fact, if the world were to end tomorrow, on Judgment Day, Arsenio Hall might be spared eternal damnation for his surprisingly great performance in *Coming to America*. Maybe.

1. "My name is Johnny Wishbone and I am a psychic from the Isle of St. Croix."
2. "Who has been puttin' their Kools out on my floor?"
3. " 'Roxanne. You don't have to put on the red light.' "
4. "I want a woman that's going to arouse my intellect as well as my loins."
5. "Did you just see a little Hare Krishna midget in a tree floatin' or is it just me?"
6. "These aren't just regular cops, okay, they're super cops, and the only things missing on these guys are capes."
7. "I ain't no punk. You try to kill me, I kill you."

1. Axel Foley in *Beverly Hills Cop II*
2. Billy Ray Valentine in *Trading Places*
3. Reggie Hammond in *48 Hrs.*
4. Prince Akeem in *Coming to America*
5. Chandler Jarrell in *The Golden Child*
6. Axel Foley in *Beverly Hills Cop*
7. Quick in *Harlem Nights*

"What do you use for a jockstrap? A peanut shell and a rubber band?"

Actually, jockstraps provided a leitmotif in this influential Canadian-made '80s "film." Think of Kim Cattrall being muzzled with one. Still confused? C'mon, you definitely saw this movie one Saturday at midnight on HBO sometime in your adolescence. It's **Porky's** of course. And the line is spoken by the wry hooker, **Cherry Forever** (Susan Clark), to the appropriately named Pee Wee. Movie critics near and far reviled *Porky's* and its incredibly juvenile sexual humor as if it were a remake of Leni Riefenstahl's *Triumph of the Will*. But if you were a fourteen-year-old boy in 1982, that shower scene was the best thing to come out of Canada since Gordie Howe.

Airplanes and Naked Guns: The Comic Genius of Zucker, Zucker, and Abrahams

No book on '80s movies would be complete without the mention of auteurs David Zucker, Jerry Zucker, and Jim Abrahams. Their four '80s collaborations were amazing. But like many collaborators, the individual projects they worked on thereafter didn't quite measure up. Let's face it, the *Hot Shots!* movies weren't much, and as for that Oscar-nominated thing Jerry Zucker directed in 1990 (Whoopi fans, you might want to turn the page right about now) . . . *Ghost* sucks.

1. "Joey, have you ever been in . . . in a Turkish prison?"
2. "In women's tennis, I always root against the heterosexual."
3. "And maybe the problems of two people don't amount to a hill of beans. But this is our hill. And these are our beans."
4. "Looks like I picked the wrong week to quit amphetamines."
5. "Same old story. Boy finds girl, boy loses girl, girl finds boy, boy forgets girl, boy remembers girl, girl dies in a tragic blimp accident over the Orange Bowl on New Year's Day."
6. "I'm being marked down? I've been kidnapped by Kmart."
7. "I know a little German. He's sitting over there."
8. "Saaaay, nice beaver."
9. "Pinch-hitting for Pedro Borbon: Manny Mota . . . Mota . . . Mota."
10. "My only regret, Carol, is that the plan isn't more violent."

1. **Captain Oveur** (Peter Graves) in *Airplane!*
2. **Blindman** (Ian McNeice) in *Top Secret!*
3. **Lieutenant Frank Drebin** (Leslie Nielsen) in *The Naked Gun: From the Files of Police Squad!*
4. **McCroskey** (Lloyd Bridges) in *Airplane!*
5. **Lieutenant Frank Drebin** (Leslie Nielsen) in *The Naked Gun: From the Files of Police Squad!*
6. **Barbara Stone** (Bette Midler) in *Ruthless People*
7. **Hillary Flammond** (Lucy Gutteridge) in *Top Secret!*
8. **Lieutenant Frank Drebin** (Leslie Nielsen) in *The Naked Gun: From the Files of Police Squad!*
9. **Ted Striker** (Robert Hays) in *Airplane!*
10. **Sam Stone** (Danny DeVito) in *Ruthless People*

"Wax on, wax off."

The director from *Rocky*. Eastern philosophy. Arnold from *Happy Days*.

No doubt about it, John G. Avildsen's **The Karate Kid** had all the trappings of a box office smash. The movie's charm owes largely to the performances of its two stars, Pat Morita and Ralph Macchio. Morita—as **Mr. Miyagi**—cuts a fine cloth of a man as the handyman/karate teacher who teaches Ralph Macchio the importance of little trees, menial labor, and the dreaded crane kick. And the Macchio Man himself showed us that he'd come a long way from playing Jeremy Andretti, the tough motherless kid with a heart of gold who moves to California in *Eight Is Enough*, by playing Daniel, the tough fatherless kid with a heart of gold who moves to California in *The Karate Kid*.

Michael, Jason, Freddie, and More: Teen Slasher Movies

slash·er flick ('slash-ər 'flik) *n*   **1:** Abhorrent film genre that blossomed in the '80s wherein a group of stereotypical adolescents are maimed and/or killed for their sexual transgressions. Multiple sequels must follow.   **2:** Any movie that borrows the plot formula of *Halloween* but replaces Michael Myers with   **a:** a chain saw–wielding madman   **b:** the lone survivor of a horrible summer camp accident   **c:** the guy who played the "friendly alien" on *V* wearing a hat and a bad-looking sweater   **3:** Any movie in which a character played by the comely Jamie Lee Curtis finds her life in peril.

Note: We've decided to include a couple of lines from bad sequels below (even though there's a bad sequels section on p. 207) because when you take the bad sequels away from the slasher flicks, you're left with about two movies. And we thought that would be a little too easy, even for fans of slasher movies.

1. "You have one choice, boy—sex or the saw. Sex is, well, nobody knows. But the saw, the saw is family!"
2. "I shot him six times! I shot him in the heart. I shot him six times."
3. "Whatever you do, don't fall asleep."
4. "In the lake, the one . . . the one who attacked me, the one who pulled me underwater."
5. "Principal by day, disco king by night."

1. **Drayton Sawyer** (Jim Siedow) in ***The Texas Chainsaw Massacre: Part 2***
2. **Sam Loomis** (Donald Pleasence) in ***Halloween II***
3. **Nancy Thompson** (Heather Langenkamp) in ***A Nightmare on Elm Street***
4. **Alice** (Adrienne King) in ***Friday the 13th***
5. **Kim** (Jamie Lee Curtis) in ***Prom Night***

"Nobody puts Baby in a corner."

What do **Dirty Dancing**, *No Way Out*, *The Principal*, and *Near Dark* have in common? Our scofflaw editor saw all four movies on the same day. No, she didn't rent them. She pulled the greatest of '80s adolescent capers: sneaking into four movies while paying for only one. Remember doing that? Sure you do.

Anyway, this line was spoken by heartthrob **Johnny Castle** (Patrick Swayze) to a pre-nose job Jennifer Grey. While women across America flocked to the theaters for this one, guys like us begged our barbers for coifs just like Johnny Castle's so we could pick up chicks who looked just like Penny Johnson.

Dance the Night Away

We'll never know why movies about dancing do incredibly well at the box office, but they do. Here are six lines from movies that featured some class of dancing. One of them even featured a woman who was a welder by day and a dancer by night. Go figure. Anyway, if you're looking for a mention of that Deney Terrio–looking Irish freak from *Lord of the Dance*, you'll have to wait for the '90s version of this book.

1. "Look, spaghetti arms. This is my dance space."
2. "Everybody else here is colorful, or eccentric, or charismatic, and I'm perfectly normal."
3. "Now, eventually it's obvious to me that she wants to do more than dance."
4. "When you give up your dreams, you die."
5. "Finally, all of Baltimore knows—I'm big, blond, and beautiful."
6. "Why, the Cabbage Patch mothers are having a PTA meeting?"

1. **Johnny Castle** (Patrick Swayze) in *Dirty Dancing*
2. **Doris** (Maureen Teefy) in *Fame*
3. **Ren** (Kevin Bacon) in *Footloose*
4. **Nick Hurley** (Michael Nouri) in *Flashdance*
5. **Tracy** (Ricki Lake) in *Hairspray*
6. **Jeff Malene** (Lee Montgomery) in *Girls Just Want to Have Fun*

"Does Barry Manilow know that you raid his wardrobe?"

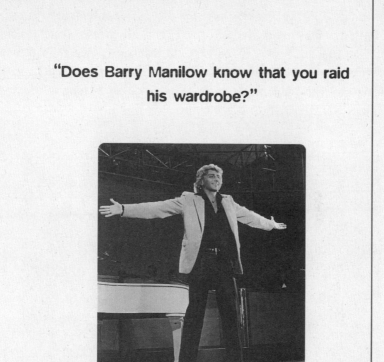

Speaking of Barry Manilow, a few years after he was thrilling his middle-aged fans with the likes of "Made It Through the Rain," John Hughes was thrilling teen moviegoers everywhere with his magnum opus, ***The Breakfast Club.*** Hughes himself actually has a cameo in the movie as Brian's father. This line was spoken by **John Bender** (Judd Nelson) to Richard Vernon, the dean of students at Shermer High. Our personal favorite role of Nelson's in the '80s was the one that didn't force us to look at that annoying sneer on his face—he did the voice of Rodimus Prime in *The Transformers: The Movie.* It's interesting to note that *The Breakfast Club* is kind of like the anti–*Fast Times at Ridgemont High.* Even though the ensemble cast did manage to live their fifteen minutes of fame to the fullest, they were pretty much relegated to B movies while Sean Penn and Jennifer Jason Leigh were being nominated for various acting awards in the '90s.

Deities of the '80s—John Hughes

John Hughes was the '80s version of Midas—and we're not talking mufflers here. Just about everything this man touched turned to gold at the box office. And rightfully so. His funny and touching teen comedies defined the '80s for many of our generation. And whether you're a Hughes fan or not, there's no denying the fact that there's something quintessentially '80s about what Hughes portrayed in *Sixteen Candles*, *The Breakfast Club*, *Ferris Bueller's Day Off*, *Some Kind of Wonderful*, and *Pretty in Pink*. Hughes was also responsible for writing the *National Lampoon Vacation* movies; *Mr. Mom*; *Planes, Trains & Automobiles*; and *The Great Outdoors*. Of course, nobody's perfect. *Weird Science*, which Hughes literally wrote in two days, effectively sank Anthony Michael Hall's career for five years. But it did feature the incredibly hot Kelly Le-Brock, who starred in just two movies before she was abducted by, uh, we mean, married to, martial *artiste* Steven Seagal.

And just for the record, Molly Ringwald, Anthony Michael Hall, and Macaulay Culkin all have Hughes to thank for their once meteoric careers.

For your reading pleasure, we've devoted the next nine pages to the movies John Hughes wrote, produced, and directed in the '80s.

1. "The question is not, What are we going to do? The question is, What *aren't* we going to do?"
2. "So, what would you little maniacs like to do first?"
3. "I'm a kid—that's my job."
4. "I'll go see where he's bivouacked the family."
5. "I'd rather be with someone for the wrong reasons than be alone for the right."
6. "Money really means nothing to me. Do you think I'd treat my parents' house this way if it did?"
7. "Hey, how come Andrew gets to get up? If he gets up, we'll all get up. It'll be anarchy!"
8. "This information cannot leave this room, okay? It would devastate my reputation as a dude."
9. "I yelled at Kenny today for coloring outside the lines."
10. "I gotta be crazy! I'm on a pilgrimage to see a moose. Praise Marty Moose!"

1. **Ferris Bueller** (Matthew Broderick) in *Ferris Bueller's Day Off*
2. **Lisa** (Kelly LeBrock) in *Weird Science*
3. **Miles Russell** (Macaulay Culkin) in *Uncle Buck*
4. **Roman** (Dan Aykroyd) in *The Great Outdoors*
5. **Amanda Jones** (Lea Thompson) in *Some Kind of Wonderful*
6. **Steff** (James Spader) in *Pretty in Pink*
7. **John Bender** (Judd Nelson) in *The Breakfast Club*
8. **The Geek/Farmer Ted** (Anthony Michael Hall) in *Sixteen Candles*
9. **Jack Butler** (Michael Keaton) in *Mr. Mom*
10. **Clark Griswold** (Chevy Chase) in *National Lampoon's Vacation*

The John Hughes Matching Game

Can you match the character with the actor?

a. Alan Ruck

b. Jon Cryer

1. **The Geek/Farmer Ted**   c. Mary Stuart Masterson

2. **Ed Rooney**   d. James Spader

3. **Blane**   e. Jeffrey Jones

4. **Allison Reynolds**   f. Gedde Watanabe

5. **Andie**   g. Anthony Michael Hall

6. **John Bender**   h. Andrew McCarthy

7. **Duckie**   i. Molly Ringwald

8. **Cameron Frye**   j. Ally Sheedy

9. **Long Duk Dong**   k. Judd Nelson

10. **Watts**

11. **Steff**

1. **g** *(Sixteen Candles)*
2. **e** *(Ferris Bueller's Day Off)*
3. **h** *(Pretty in Pink)*
4. **j** *(The Breakfast Club)*
5. **i** *(Pretty in Pink)*
6. **k** *(The Breakfast Club)*
7. **b** *(Pretty in Pink)*
8. **a** *(Ferris Bueller's Day Off)*
9. **f** *(Sixteen Candles)*
10. **c** *(Some Kind of Wonderful)*
11. **d** *(Pretty in Pink)*

1. "It must be a drag to be a slave to the male sex drive."
2. "People don't mature anymore. They stay jackasses all their lives."
3. "You do more ballhandling in one minute than Larry Bird does in an hour."
4. "Pardon my French, but you're an asshole!"
5. "We're all in this together. This is a full-blown, four-alarm holiday emergency here."
6. "Chicks cannot hold their smoke. That's what it is."
7. "That's why they call them crushes. If they were easy, they'd call them something else."
8. "Big Ben, kids, Parliament."

1. **Watts** (Mary Stuart Masterson) in *Some Kind of Wonderful*
2. **Grandfather** (Bill Erwin) in *She's Having a Baby*
3. **Del Griffith** (John Candy) in *Planes, Trains & Automobiles*
4. **Cameron Frye** (Alan Ruck) in *Ferris Bueller's Day Off*
5. **Clark Griswold** (Chevy Chase) in *National Lampoon's Christmas Vacation*
6. **Brian Johnson** (Anthony Michael Hall) in *The Breakfast Club*
7. **Jim Baker** (Paul Dooley) in *Sixteen Candles*
8. **Clark Griswold** (Chevy Chase) in *National Lampoon's European Vacation*

"Oh, he's very popular, Ed. The sportos, the motorheads, geeks, sluts, bloods, waistoids, dweebies, dickheads—they all adore him. They think he's a righteous dude."

The actress who spoke this line, Edie McClurg, has been in a surprising number of cool projects in her career. Among her credits she counts *Carrie*, *The Pee-Wee Herman Show*, *Mr. Mom*, two Cheech and Chong movies, *WKRP in Cincinnati*, and the short-lived existential TV sketch comedy show *No Soap, Radio*. But the start of her acting career wasn't quite so hip. She was a regular on the *Tony Orlando and Dawn* variety show (egad!).

McClurg as **Grace**, the principal's secretary, is just one piece of many that fit together to make ***Ferris Bueller's Day Off*** one of John Hughes's biggest successes. And even if you're one of the few people on this planet who didn't like this movie, you have to admit that any movie whose soundtrack features the Beatles' "Twist and Shout," Wayne Newton's "Danke Schoen," and Yello's "Oh Yeah" is worth seeing.

Deities of the '80s—Jack Nicholson

What is there possibly left to say about Jack Nicholson? We could tell you that he was born in Neptune, New Jersey, and make some joke about the planet or the stench on the Garden State Parkway, but belittling Jack would be like insulting your best friend's mom. You just don't do it (unless of course your friend's mom really liked the Nicholson-penned *Head*, then we guess it's okay to insult Jack a little bit). After a spate of B movies, Jack broke out in *Easy Rider* and instantly became one of Hollywood's biggest stars. In the '80s, Jack was nominated for four Oscars, winning one for his role as the aging, overweight Garrett Breedlove in the film adaptation of Larry McMurtry's *Terms of Endearment*. Now that's all we're going to say about Jack. If you want some lame joke about his pie-eyed escapades in a run-down Jamaica, Queens, liquor store, watch a Jay Leno monologue or something.

1. "Did you ever dance with the devil in the pale moonlight?"
2. "Do you think God knew what he was doing when he created woman?"
3. "This is a brutal layoff. And all because they couldn't program Wednesday nights."
4. "Scabs deserve what they get."
5. "Does your sister behave like this at all of her weddings?"
6. "Do I ice her? Do I marry her? Which one of these?"
7. "I was just inches from a clean getaway."
8. " 'No more' does not mean more, and more, and more. 'No more' means no more."
9. "If you were mine I wouldn't share you with anybody or anything."
10. "I'm not gonna hurt ya. I'm just gonna bash your brains in."

1. **Jack Napier/The Joker** in *Batman*
2. **Daryl Van Horne** in *The Witches of Eastwick*
3. **Bill Rorich** in *Broadcast News*
4. **Francis Phelan** in *Ironweed*
5. **Mark** in *Heartburn*
6. **Charley Partanna** in *Prizzi's Honor*
7. **Garrett Breedlove** in *Terms of Endearment*
8. **Charlie Smith** in *The Border*
9. **Eugene O'Neill** in *Reds*
10. **Jack Torrance** in *The Shining*

All Mixed Up, Part II

1. "Awesome amounts of alliteration from anxious anchors placed in powerful posts."
2. "Frankly, Scarlett, I don't give a damn."
3. "I think that time is like a burrito, in the sense that one part of itself will fold over and it will just touch the other part."
4. "I always tell the truth. Even when I lie."
5. "Truthfully, don't you find being a woman in the eighties complicated?"
6. "So if you can't take pride in your job, remember, there's always work at the post office."
7. "That's not a knife. *That's* a knife."
8. "Do we really hurt them by killing them?"
9. "Here's a picture of my sister. If you let us go you can have her. I hear she's quite good."
10. "This place has a sign hanging over the urinal that says, 'Don't eat the big white mint.' "
11. "I'm like a wife. I'm like a boring, clinging, miserable little wife."
12. "The problem is that Lou's aunt works the cash register and his sister's the hostess."
13. "If you don't let me out I'm throwing up all over the front seat."
14. "I was once a shameless, full-time dope fiend."
15. "That's not a dress you wear to a wedding. That's a dress you wear to a hooker's wedding."
16. "It's not my goddamn planet; understand, monkey boy?"
17. "Tough guys don't do math. Tough guys fry chicken for a living."
18. "Badgers? Badgers? We don't need no stinking badgers."

1. **Aaron Altman** (Albert Brooks) in *Broadcast News*
2. **Wadsworth** (Tim Curry) in *Clue*
3. **Richard Norvik** (Barry Miller) in *Peggy Sue Got Married*
4. **Tony Montana** (Al Pacino) in *Scarface*
5. **Julie** (Jessica Lange) in *Tootsie*
6. **Bobby Taylor** (Robert Townsend) in *Hollywood Shuffle*
7. **Michael J. "Crocodile" Dundee** (Paul Hogan) in *Crocodile Dundee*
8. **Anthony Castelo** (Dan Hedaya) in *Wise Guys*
9. **Emmett Fitz-Hume** (Chevy Chase) in *Spies Like Us*
10. **Wade Garrett** (Sam Elliott) in *Road House*
11. **Louise Bryant** (Diane Keaton) in *Reds*
12. **Sunny Davis** (Goldie Hawn) in *Protocol*
13. **Putter** (Yeardley Smith) in *The Legend of Billie Jean*
14. **Bob** (Matt Dillon) in *Drugstore Cowboy*
15. **Aunt Sofia** (Gina de Angeles) in *Cousins*
16. **John Bigboote** (Christopher Lloyd) in *The Adventures of Buckaroo Banzai Across the Eighth Dimension*
17. **Jaime Escalante** (Edward James Olmos) in *Stand and Deliver*
18. **Raul Hernandez** (Trinidad Silva) in *UHF*

"There's things about me you don't know, Dottie. Things you wouldn't understand. Things you couldn't understand. Things you shouldn't understand."

If you were expecting a masturbation joke here, go buy our first book, *Who Can It Be Now?*, and check out the Wham!/George Michael section. There will be no . . . we repeat . . . *no* **Pee-Wee Herman** bashing in our book. If you played a lovable, winsome, slightly confused freak of a boy for your whole life, wouldn't you need some sort of release, too? So Paul Reubens, aka Pee-Wee Herman, was arrested in 1991 in the great state of Florida for doing you know what. Big deal. That does not take away from his genius '80s accomplishments. The Pee-Wee Herman legacy began in 1981 when HBO aired the brilliant sketch comedy *The Pee-Wee Herman Show*, which, incidentally, costarred the late Phil Hartman. In 1985, Tim Burton directed ***Pee-Wee's Big Adventure*** and effectively launched the little weirdo's career. Two other movies and an award-winning children's show followed. And if you didn't weep at the part in *Pee-Wee's Big Adventure* when Pee-Wee finds out that the Alamo doesn't have a basement, then you're a cold, heartless human being.

"I know you are but what am I?"

Deities of the '80s—Arnold Schwarzenegger

This native of Graz, Austria, and former bodybuilding champion carved quite a nice little niche for himself in Hollywood. He traded in performing alongside muscleheads like Franco Columbu and Sergio Oliva to get to work alongside women like Linda Hamilton (what did she ever see in James Cameron anyway?) and Penelope Ann Miller. Not too bad. Of all Arnold's cinematic efforts in the '80s, *Predator* stands out as the best. It's got a classic action-movie plot and a great supporting cast, including Carl Weathers, who played Apollo Creed in seven or eight Rocky movies, and Jesse "the Body" Ventura, future Minnesota governor and former archrival of longtime WWF champion Bob Backlund.

Arnold's most famous movie quote is "I'll be back." The reason you won't find it here is because it appeared in *five* of his '80s movies. They are *The Terminator*, *Commando*, *Predator*, *The Running Man*, and *Twins*.

1. "I'm not into politics. I'm into survival."
2. "To crush your enemies, see them driven before you, and to hear the lamentation of the women."
3. "I do not want to touch his ass, I want to make him talk."
4. "If it bleeds, we can kill it."
5. "Nice night for a walk."
6. "What do you think I look like, Dirty Harry?"
7. "Thank you for the cookies. I look forward to tossing them."
8. "You're a funny guy, Sully. I like you. That's why I'm going to kill you last."
9. "I'm no mercenary. Nobody pays me. And if I think somebody owes me something, I take it."

1. **Ben Richards** in *The Running Man*
2. **Conan** in *Conan the Barbarian*
3. **Ivan Danko** in *Red Heat*
4. **Dutch** in *Predator*
5. **Terminator** in *The Terminator*
6. **Kaminski** in *Raw Deal*
7. **Julius Benedict** in *Twins*
8. **Matrix** in *Commando*
9. **Kalidor** in *Red Sonja*

"When will they ever listen? When will they ever learn?"

Clash of the Titans should be required viewing in every high-school Latin class in America. What better way is there to learn about mythology? Forget what anybody says against it—this was a fun movie. A woman who turns men to stone, talking statues, flying horses (who was Pegasus' sire anyway?)—what more could you possibly want?

And then there was the cast. Okay, so in retrospect, Laurence Olivier as Zeus was probably not his proudest moment as an actor, but who else were they going to get to play the king of the gods? A long-haired Harry Hamlin made a fine Perseus, and he didn't have to make any of those self-righteous speeches like he did in *L.A. Law*. And, best of all, the hottest Bond girl ever, Ursula Andress, got plenty of screen time as Aphrodite. The line from the preceding page was spoken by **Ammon** (Burgess Meredith) as he opined the fate of humankind.

Girls Just Wanna Have Fun: The Most Memorable Female Characters of the Decade

Whether you were a fan of the tall, muscular Lieutenant Ellen Ripley kicking butt in *Aliens* or the ruddy, innocent Samantha lamenting unrequited love in *Sixteen Candles*, you have to admit that the '80s were chock-full of some pretty righteous leading ladies. Here are lines from our favorite female characters of the decade. And don't worry, there are no lines here from Charlie (Wendy O. Williams) in *Reform School Girls*.

1. "To call you stupid would be an insult to stupid people."
2. "Captain, being held by you isn't quite enough to get me excited."
3. "That'll never be me, that'll never be me. That'll never be, never be me. No!"
4. "In time you'll drop dead and I'll come to your funeral in a red dress."
5. "You don't know what it's like being a woman looking the way I do."
6. "Do I look like the mother of the future?"
7. "You know what I want? Cool guys like you out of my life."
8. "Have you ever done it in an elevator?"
9. "Most women at one time or another have faked it."
10. "I'm scared of walking out of this room and never feeling the rest of my whole life the way I feel when I'm with you."
11. "And we are your friends, Angela, whether you like it or not."
12. "Tear down that bitch of a bearing wall, and put a window where it ought to be."
13. "Gimme that baby, you warthog from hell."
14. "He eats cheese balls and beer for breakfast."
15. "I was a better man with you as a woman than I ever was with a woman as a man."

1. **Wanda** (Jamie Lee Curtis) in *A Fish Called Wanda*
2. **Princess Leia** (Carrie Fisher) in *The Empire Strikes Back*
3. **Corey Flood** (Lili Taylor) in *Say Anything . . .*
4. **Loretta Castorini** (Cher) in *Moonstruck*
5. **Jessica Rabbit** (Kathleen Turner) in *Who Framed Roger Rabbit*
6. **Sarah Connor** (Linda Hamilton) in *The Terminator*
7. **Veronica Sawyer** (Winona Ryder) in *Heathers*
8. **Alex Forrest** (Glenn Close) in *Fatal Attraction*
9. **Sally Allbright** (Meg Ryan) in *When Harry Met Sally . . .*
10. **Frances "Baby" Houseman** (Jennifer Grey) in *Dirty Dancing*
11. **Connie Russo** (Mercedes Ruehl) in *Married to the Mob*
12. **Joan Crawford** (Faye Dunaway) in *Mommie Dearest*
13. **Ed** (Holly Hunter) in *Raising Arizona*
14. **Alison Bradbury** (Daphne Zuniga) in *The Sure Thing*
15. **Dorothy Michaels/Michael Dorsey** (Dustin Hoffman) in *Tootsie*

Ah yes, the age-old question: Who gives more boring, self-important acceptance speeches, actors or directors? To answer, let's envision a fight to the death between two notorious offenders. In this corner, in the purple trunks, weighing in at 170 pounds (160 of which are his ego) director James "King of the World" Cameron. And, in this corner, wearing the modified habit of a Carmelite nun, weighing in at 120 pounds, actress Sally "You like me! You really like me!" Field.

Who would win?

a. Cameron
b. Field
c. Movie audiences everywhere

1. "Why should I be happy about being a grandmother?"
2. "Forgive me, Your Majesty. I am a vulgar man, but my music is not."
3. "I believe that God made me for a purpose—for China. But he also made me fast."
4. "It's not her fault, Baroness. She's a lion."
5. "An eye for an eye only ends up making the whole world blind."
6. "A little advice about feeling, kiddo. Don't expect it always to tickle."
7. "Mama, cars don't behave. They are behaved upon."
8. "Death. What do you all know about death?"
9. "I'm an excellent driver."
10. "Your Majesty, in my country it would be usual to begin with some kind of an examination."

1. **Aurora Greenway** (Shirley MacLaine) in *Terms of Endearment*
2. **Wolfgang Amadeus Mozart** (Tom Hulce) in *Amadeus*
3. **Eric Liddell** (Ian Charleson) in *Chariots of Fire*
4. **Denys Finch Hatton** (Robert Redford) in *Out of Africa*
5. **Mohandas Gandhi** (Ben Kingsley) in *Gandhi*
6. **Dr. Berger** (Judd Hirsch) in *Ordinary People*
7. **Boolie Werthan** (Dan Aykroyd) in *Driving Miss Daisy*
8. **Sergeant Barnes** (Tom Berenger) in *Platoon*
9. **Raymond Babbitt** (Dustin Hoffman) in *Rain Man*
10. **Reginald Johnston** (Peter O'Toole) in *The Last Emperor*

"These things are good: ice cream and cake, a ride on a Harley, seeing monkeys in the trees, the rain on my tongue, and the sun shining on my face."

Basically, if Little Orphan Annie married the Elephant Man and produced a hideously deformed child, **Rocky Dennis** would be it. Directed by Peter Bogdanovich and starring Cher, Sam Elliott, Laura Dern, and Eric Stoltz, *Mask* tells the story of a warm, friendly, intelligent teenager who is born with a head the size of a buffalo's. The movie won an Oscar for Best Makeup (you should see what they did to Cher), and it tugged at the heartstrings of '80s moviegoers everywhere. Cher, who plays Rusty Dennis, Rocky's mother, solidified her burgeoning big-screen career with a memorable performance.

Incidentally, Eric Stoltz, who plays the craniodiaphyseal dysplasiac teen, was slated to play Marty McFly in *Back to the Future* but was fired for failing to act like a teenager. This opened the door for the ever-youthful Michael J. Fox, who transformed himself from being just Alex P. Keaton on TV's *Family Ties* into a big-screen star.

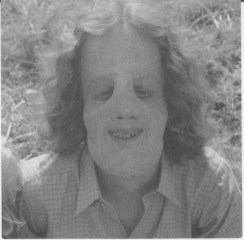

Deities of the '80s—Michelle Pfeiffer

We used to think Michelle Pfeiffer was pretty cool until we found out she used to date Fisher Stevens—you know, the actor who played that Indian guy in *Short Circuit*. But despite that, Pfeiffer was responsible for a handful of decent characters in the '80s. The former Miss Orange County beauty pageant winner has been gainfully employed ever since she landed her first speaking part on television's *Fantasy Island*. And while she's gone on to even greater stardom in the '90s, we will always remember her as Suzie Q in the incredibly funny, incredibly juvenile *The Hollywood Knights* and as Stephanie in *Grease 2*. Here are a handful of movies Pfeiffer graced in the '80s. Thankfully, her appearance in Coolio's video for "Gangsta's Paradise" was in the '90s, so we don't have to say anything about that here. Ooops.

1. "I mean, does anybody really need to hear 'Feelings' again in their lifetime?"
2. "Everything we wear, everything we own, fell off a truck."
3. "So I promise: No more refusals, no more regrets."
4. "You need some Chapstick or something 'cause your lips keep getting stuck on your teeth."
5. "I don't understand why there has to be any pain."
6. "Don't toot your horn, honey, you're not that good."
7. "I'm free every day. It's in the Constitution."

1. **Susie Diamond** in *The Fabulous Baker Boys*
2. **Angela DeMarco** in *Married to the Mob*
3. **Madame de Tourval** in *Dangerous Liaisons*
4. **Jo Ann Vallenari** in *Tequila Sunrise*
5. **Sukie Ridgemont** in *The Witches of Eastwick*
6. **Elvira** in *Scarface*
7. **Stephanie** in *Grease 2*

"I don't want to sell anything, buy anything, or process anything as a career. I
don't want to sell anything bought or
processed, or buy anything sold or
processed, or process anything sold,
bought, or processed, or repair anything
sold, bought, or processed. You know, as
a career, I don't want to do that."

Cameron Crowe's ***Say Anything . . .*** didn't make a big splash at the box office, but it remains one of the most enduring movies to emerge from the whole decade. We could go on and on about the reasons for its success but we want to offer up a reason nobody's thought of yet—kickboxing.

Lloyd Dobler (John Cusack) calls it "the sport of the future." His idol is kickboxing champion Don "the Dragon" Wilson—and if there's one thing Lloyd wants other than to be with Diane, it's to be a professional kickboxer.[*] We firmly believe that the moviegoing population's growing infatuation with martial arts had something to do with the success of this picture. Forget the scene where John Mahoney sings along to "Rikki Don't Lose That Number" or the boom box scene with Peter Gabriel's "In Your Eyes," nothing gets an audience good and riled up like a roundhouse kick. We have to admit, though, Cusack pulls off an even more impressive maneuver—he's so likable that *Say Anything . . .* is a romantic comedy that even men will watch.

[*]The Dragon actually makes an appearance in the film as Lloyd's sparring partner.

Jake LaMotta, Rupert Pupkin, and Jesus Christ: Martin Scorsese in the '80s

Martin Scorsese is nothing if not demanding on his actors. Take *Raging Bull*. He has Robert De Niro gain fifty pounds to play Jake LaMotta. But at least asking someone to travel around Tuscany gorging himself on pasta has an upside. Look at poor Joe Pesci—he breaks a rib in a sparring scene and Scorsese doesn't even bother to tell him that De Niro's going to attack him on camera in the famous "Did you f**k my wife?" scene. We guess it still beats waiting tables at Amici's on 187th Street.

Whatever Scorsese does, it works. *Raging Bull* and *The King of Comedy* are two of our top five '80s movies, and we could probably fill a whole book of quotes from just them and 1990's *GoodFellas*. ("I never agreed to three points above the vig." Sorry. We had to get that in there.)

1. "You never got me down, Ray. You hear me? You never got me down."
2. "Ma! I'm trying to make a recording!"
3. "What do you want from me? I'm just a word processor!"
4. "We got a racehorse here, a thoroughbred. You make him feel good, I teach him how to run."
5. "What's good for man isn't good for God."

1. **Jake LaMotta** (Robert De Niro) in *Raging Bull*
2. **Rupert Pupkin** (Robert De Niro) in *The King of Comedy*
3. **Paul Hackett** (Griffin Dunne) in *After Hours*
4. **Eddie Felson** (Paul Newman) in *The Color of Money*
5. **Judas** (Harvey Keitel) in *The Last Temptation of Christ*

"Bring it over!"

"We came, we saw, we kicked its ass."

Who you gonna call? **Dr. Peter Venkman** (Bill Murray) and his *Ghostbusters* cronies or Agent Fox Mulder of *The X-Files*? It's a tough call, but here's the tale of the tape. It's up to you to decide the Parapsychologist Champion of the Universe.

Partners
A handful of overweight, balding, nerdy men
or
A redheaded goddess who makes Sigourney Weaver look like Dian Fossey

Perk of the Job
Makes out with a woman possessed by the demon god Zuul
or
Has sex with a gorgeous but murderous vampire

Career Setbacks
Unconventional research techniques get him kicked out of Columbia University
or
Unconventional theories get him fired and rehired more times than Billy Martin

Equipment
Bad jumpsuit and unlicensed nuclear proton accelerator
or
Cellular telephone and semiautomatic handgun

Archenemy
The Sta-Puf Marshmallow Man
or
The Cigarette-Smoking Man

Experience
Two feature-length movies and an animated television series
or
One feature-length movie and more than 135 episodes over six seasons

Theme Song
Ray Parker Jr.'s chef d'oeuvre
or
Mark Snow's haunting theme music

Notable achievement
With help from partners, prevents Gozer the Destroyer from annihilating New York City
or
With help from partner, evades death by bullet, alien, vampire, shadow government, prehistoric parasite, Chupacabra, virus-carrying bees, poltergeist, sea monster, feral woman, fluke man, liver-eating serial killer, et al.

Unless you're talking about *The Godfather* or *Jaws*, the movie is never as good as the book. But who can ignore these Hollywood adaptations? If the thought of revisiting the '80s writings of Jay McInerney or Bret Easton Ellis gives you the shivers, we empathize wholeheartedly.

1. "There's a certain shabby nobility in failing all by myself."
2. "There's gonna be sex and violence."
3. "Okay, I'll call Betty Ford—you want me to get him a room, fine."
4. "I mean, I had mine removed surgically under general anesthesia. But to have it bitten off . . . it's a nightmare."
5. "If one does what God does enough times, one will become as God is."
6. "Promise me I can have your head when the breath has left your body."
7. "Greasers will still be Greasers and Socs will still be Socs. It doesn't matter."
8. "Life is very heavy to me, and it is so light to you."
9. "I've succeeded because I've always known I was born to dominate your sex and avenge my own."
10. "I'm beginning to think that maybe it's not just how much you love someone."

1. **Jamie Conway** (Michael J. Fox) in *Bright Lights, Big City* (Jay McInerney)
2. **Lilly** (Jennie Dundas) in *The Hotel New Hampshire* (John Irving)
3. **Clay** (Andrew McCarthy) in *Less Than Zero* (Bret Easton Ellis)
4. **Roberta Muldoon** (John Lithgow) in *The World According to Garp* (John Irving)
5. **Hannibal Lecktor** (Brian Cox) in *Manhunter**
6. **Professor Andreev** (Ian McDiarmid) in *Gorky Park* (Martin Cruz Smith)
7. **Randy Anderson** (Darren Dalton) in *The Outsiders* (S. E. Hinton)
8. **Tereza** (Juliette Binoche) in *The Unbearable Lightness of Being* (Milan Kundera)
9. **Marquise de Merteuil** (Glenn Close) in *Dangerous Liaisons* (Choderlos de Laclos)
10. **Macon Leary** (William Hurt) in *The Accidental Tourist* (Anne Tyler)

*Manhunter was actually an adaptation of Thomas Harris's *Red Dragon*, the first book in which his character Hannibal Lecter appears. Proving once again that Hollywood producers can't read, they greenlighted this spelling instead.

"Strange things are afoot at the
Circle-K."

In an early 1990s casting call for Bernardo Bertolucci's *Little Buddha*, Keanu Reeves was given a giant paper bag and was told to act his way out of it. A few hours later, a mesmerized Bertolucci watched on as Keanu Reeves managed to extricate himself from the bag by uttering the words *dude* and *party on* about seven hundred times. It was a feat the great Italian director had never witnessed before. Reeves got the part as Siddhartha, and *Little Buddha* tanked at the box office. The concept of a perpetual man-child—whose most memorable role was **Ted Logan** in ***Bill & Ted's Excellent Adventure***—playing an enlightened deity makes absolutely no sense to us. Charlie Sheen said it best: "Bertolucci looks at him and says, 'That's my guy!'?"

For a time in the '80s, Debra Winger (no relation to loser metalhead Kip) was one of the biggest stars in Hollywood—she even helped provide the voice of E.T. She was nominated for Best Actress twice despite her tendency to infuriate her costars. Perhaps her reputation as being difficult to work with goes back to her brief stint as a soldier in the Israeli army. If your previous job required toting an Uzi, would you have the patience to listen to Richard "I'm down with the Lama" Gere tell you that you missed your cue?

Debra has managed some success in the past few years, including another Oscar nomination for *Shadowlands*, but for most of the '90s you were more likely to see her gracing the cover of *The Star* with Bob Kerrey or Timothy Hutton than sitting expectantly in the Dorothy Chandler Pavilion.

1. "My legs are sweatin', Mama."
2. "I even tried taxi driving once—just couldn't take it."
3. "So, Zach, what do you do with a girl when you're through with her, huh?"
4. "That's the first time I stopped hugging first."
5. "Which part do you figure a woman isn't up to, the seduction or the murder?"
6. "That look in your eyes—pure blue steel."
7. "I'll give you something. He named his dog after Ronald Reagan."

1. **Sissy** in *Urban Cowboy*
2. **Suzy** in *Cannery Row*
3. **Paula** in *An Officer and a Gentleman*
4. **Emma Horton** in *Terms of Endearment*
5. **Alexandra** in *Black Widow*
6. **Laura Kelly** in *Legal Eagles*
7. **Katie Phillips/Cathy Weaver** in *Betrayed*

"Of course you're confused. You're wearing my underwear."

Who is Billy Zabka?
Let us tell you.

William Zabka is the quintessential '80s teen-movie bad guy—the Lee Van Cleef of his day. His boring blond good looks and cocky demeanor made him the perfect antagonist to any number of '80s good guys. We're big fans of Zabka's, but even if you don't like him, you've got to admire his consistency. He played a pretty boy jock who got punched in the mouth and made a bewildered facial expression in three '80s classics, *The Karate Kid*, *Back to School*, and ***Just One of the Guys***. This line is from the latter movie (and is spoken by **Buddy**, who is played by Billy Jayne), which rates as one of the great cable movies of all time. In fact, if you go turn on USA right now, there's a 73 percent chance it'll be on.

The Best '80s Movies to Star at Least One Pro Wrestler Matching Game

The idea here is to match the wrestler or manager with the film he or she appeared in. Please note that wrestlers are very talented people and many have appeared in more than one movie. If your favorite movie starring a wrestler isn't listed here, fear not. It may well be listed in another part of the book.

1. **Ric Flair**

2. **Jesse "the Body" Ventura**

3. **Rowdy Roddy Piper**

4. **Hulk Hogan**

5. **Andy Kaufman**

6. **Captain Lou Albano**

7. **Cyndi Lauper**

8. **Dusty Rhodes**

9. **André the Giant**

10. **King Kong Bundy**

11. **Bret "the Hitman" Hart**

a. *Vibes*

b. *Rocky III*

c. *Wise Guys*

d. *It's My Turn*

e. *The Princess Bride*

f. *Buy & Cell*

g. *Body Slam*

h. *Moving*

i. *Honey, I Shrunk the Kids*

j. *The Running Man*

k. *My Breakfast with Blassie*

It's a little-known fact that the Fabulous Moolah tried out for Meryl Streep's part in *Sophie's Choice*. It's an actual fact that this statement is false.

1. **g**
2. **j**
3. **f**
4. **b**
5. **k**
6. **c**

7. **a**
8. **d**
9. **e**
10. **h**
11. **i**

A rare moment: Hogan with hair and T sans chains.

*This one is so tough (at least for guys) that
we thought we'd give you a bit of dialogue.*

Lady A: "I shall never forgive myself."

Lady B: "You always say that, Charlotte.
And then you always do forgive yourself."

Give up, fellas?

Maybe that's because no male actually saw this movie. This exchange of dialogue is between **Charlotte Bartlett** (Maggie Smith) and **Lucy Honeychurch** (Helena Bonham Carter) in Ismail Merchant and James Ivory's *A Room with a View*.

If you're not familiar with Merchant and Ivory, they're the folks who brought us such critically acclaimed pictures as *Howards End* and *The Remains of the Day*. Fans of the duo describe their movies as deliberately paced (read: slower than a claimer at Great Barrington Fair) and full of wit and elegance (read: British). But the reality for many is that if Yawn and Snore had a child, Merchant and Ivory would have made one helluva baby-sitter.

Deities of the '80s—Mel Gibson

Certain people seem so impressed that Mel Gibson, an "Australian," can do such a good American accent. News flash: He lived the first twelve years of his life in Peekskill, New York. It is rumored that in the late '60s, his father moved his family to Sydney, Australia, after winning on *Jeopardy!* Though we're not impressed by Mel's American patois, we are impressed by his past performances. He was pretty spectacular in the Mad Max movies, and we have to give him credit for not cracking up every time the diminutive Linda Hunt (playing a man—what a stretch!) uttered something incomprehensible in *The Year of Living Dangerously.* So let's go Down Under and see what Smokin' Mel was up to in the '80s.

1. "Guys like you don't die on toilets."
2. "Just looking at you hurts more."
3. "That's a real badge, I'm a real cop, and this is a real gun."
4. "I was a cop, a driver."
5. "If I mess it up they'll send me back to the newsroom in Sydney—and that's a bloody graveyard."
6. "If it's all the same to you, I'll drive that tanker."
7. "Oh, that's lovely. We put our lives in the hands of a mother parrot."

1. **Martin Riggs** in *Lethal Weapon 2*
2. **Dale McKussic** in *Tequila Sunrise*
3. **Martin Riggs** in *Lethal Weapon*
4. **Max** in *Mad Max Beyond Thunderdome*
5. **Guy Hamilton** in *The Year of Living Dangerously*
6. **Max** in *Mad Max 2*
7. **Frank Dunne** in *Gallipoli*

"And there I saw the most disgusting
thing I've ever seen in my life...
Hollyfeld in his pajamas."

There aren't many fancy gems in Val Kilmer's '80s movie-career crown, but we've gotta give him one for **Real Genius.** Val plays **Chris Knight**, a college rebel who teaches the high school prodigy Mitch Taylor* how to be cool in college, how to score with '80s bimbos, and how to turn the evil Professor Hathaway's house into a smoldering Jiffy Pop popcorn maker. Val's other '80s movie credits include *Top Gun*, *Kill Me Again* (if they'd only gotten it right the first time we wouldn't have had to sit through *Willow*) and the appropriately titled TV movie *One Too Many*. In fact, when you watch *Real Genius*, we strongly recommend you drink at least one too many to enhance your viewing pleasure.

[*Poor "Gabriel Jarrett" [*sic*], who played Taylor: Not only did his career never get off the ground, but they also didn't spell his name right in the credits. It should have only one *t*.]

The King of Kings

You thought this section was going to be about George Lucas, didn't you? Well, George certainly was a king of kings in the '80s, but he wasn't *the* king of kings. Stephen King (and his alter ego Richard Bachman) had seven of his novels and eight of his stories adapted for the big screen—one of them even starred Herman Munster. Cool!

1. "That's where I buried my dog Spot when he died of old age in 1924."
2. "I warn you I get sick. Car sick, air sick. And I'm going to throw up all over you."
3. "I ain't never seen a hero with his ass in the air like that."
4. "I was twelve going on thirteen the first time I saw a dead human being."
5. "His throat was cut deliberately. He was already dead when he stumbled out into the road."
6. "The missiles are flying. Hallelujah!"
7. "Hey, don't think you got the gold key to the crapper."
8. "Some places are like people—some shine and some don't."

1. **Mr. Crandall** (Fred Gwynne) in *Pet Sematary*
2. **Amber Mendez** (Maria Conchita Alonso) in *The Running Man*
3. **Brett** (Laura Harrington) in *Maximum Overdrive*
4. **The Writer** (Richard Dreyfuss) in *Stand by Me*
5. **Burt** (Peter Horton) in *Children of the Corn*
6. **Greg Stillson** (Martin Sheen) in *The Dead Zone*
7. **Will Darnell** (Robert Prosky) in *Christine*
8. **Dick Hallorann** (Scatman Crothers) in *The Shining*

"All work and no play makes Jack a dull boy."

"Stay gold."

What a cast! The Karate Kid, the Drugstore Cowboy, the Soul Man, the Mighty Duck, Johnny Castle, Youngblood, and Jerry Maguire.* Based on the S. E. Hinton novel of the same name, and directed by Francis Ford Coppola, the punks from **The Outsiders** became instant pinups on every teenage girl's locker in America. And though the movie is filled with memorable quotes—"We'll do it for Johnny" being the most memorable of them—we chose this one simply because the concept of **Johnny** (Ralph Macchio) quoting Robert Frost and telling Pony Boy (C. Thomas Howell) to "stay gold" seemed a tad bit ironic to us. You too?

*Ralph Macchio, Matt Dillon, C. Thomas Howell, Emilio Estevez, Patrick Swayze, Rob Lowe, and Tom Cruise made up the fabled Greasers. Their archenemies, the Socs (pronounced So-shhhs) featured Leif Garrett. Tom Waits had a bit part as Dallas's (Matt Dillon) friend Buck Merrill. We don't know about you, but we'd take Tom Waits in a real knife fight against any one of those pretty boys—Leif Garrett included.

Other than Bruce Springsteen, Meryl Streep was the most popular New Jersey native of the '80s (sorry Jon Bon Jovi). Not only did she win two Academy Awards (granted, one of them was for the 1979 movie *Kramer vs. Kramer*), but she was also nominated for five others. Despite these accolades, this fine actress will forever be linked to the delivery of one of the most melodramatic lines in cinematic history. Do you know what line and which movie we're talking about? Okay, we'll give you a few hints: a true story set in the Australian outback; based on the book *Evil Angels* by John Bryson; Elaine Benes (Julia-Louis Dreyfus) uttered a variation of the line to an annoying Australian woman in a now-famous episode of *Seinfeld*. Well, you should know the line and the movie by now.[*] The movie is 1988's *A Cry in the Dark*. And the overwrought, overdramatic line is (please say with a faux-Australian accent): *"The dingo's got my baby!"*

1. "A stimulated accountant sounds very interesting."
2. "We're talking about my baby daughter, not some object."
3. "You probably think it very bourgeois to cook for someone on the first date."
4. "When the gods want to punish you they answer your prayers."
5. "It says here that plutonium gives you cancer."
6. "This ridiculous language—there's too many words."
7. "He told me I was beautiful but he could not understand why I was not married."

[*]If you didn't know the line or the movie, then you probably didn't know that Meryl Streep was once engaged to John Cazale (Fredo!) either.

1. **Mary Fisher** in *She-Devil*
2. **Lindy Chamberlain** in *A Cry in the Dark*
3. **Rachel** in *Heartburn*
4. **Karen Blixen-Finecke** in *Out of Africa*
5. **Karen Silkwood** in *Silkwood*
6. **Sophie Zawistowska** in *Sophie's Choice*
7. **Sarah** in *The French Lieutenant's Woman*

"I know it was you, Fredo. You broke my heart. You broke my heart."

"I want an official Red Ryder, carbine action, two-hundred-shot range model air rifle!"

"You'll shoot your eye out, kid" was the familiar refrain every time **Ralphie** (played by Peter Billingsley) asked for a Red Ryder BB gun. His teacher, his mother, and even a surreal Santa Claus discouraged Ralphie from getting his dream toy. But the Old Man (Darren McGavin) fulfills Ralphie's wish and buys him the coveted air rifle. Of course, Ralphie nearly shoots his eye out with the first shot he fires. *A Christmas Story*, based on Jean Shepherd's brilliant collection *In God We Trust, All Others Pay Cash*, is *the* Christmas movie for the '80s generation—it's incredibly funny, it's charming, and more important, it confirms the suburban myth that if you lick a metal pole in freezing winter weather, your tongue will stick there forever—or at least until a rescue crew arrives.

"How about a nice football?" Ho. Ho. Ho.

How about a Fresca? Lines from *Caddyshack*

With an all-star cast that included Chevy Chase, Rodney Dangerfield, Ted Knight, and Bill Murray, *Caddyshack* jump-started the golf movie genre. It's strange that we haven't heard more from Michael O'Keefe since his character Danny Noonan won the caddy tournament in dramatic fashion. Sure, in the early '90s he married Bonnie Raitt and landed a role on *Roseanne*, but we hardly call those major accomplishments. We thought this guy was going to be a movie star, but they didn't even drag him out for *Caddyshack II*. Even the guy who played Noonan's archrival, Tony D'Annunzio (Scott Colomby), had more of a big-screen career. At least he appeared in a few of the *Porky's* movies. Can you guess which characters said these lines?

1. "It's easy to grin when your ship comes in."
2. "So I got that goin' for me—which is nice."
3. "Hey, you're a funny kid, you know. What time you due back in Boys Town?"
4. "She's been plucked more times than the Rose of Tralee—biggest whore on Fifth Avenue, I'm told."
5. "Never ask a Navy man if he'll have another drink, 'cause it's nobody's goddamned business how many drinks he's had already."

1. **Judge Smails** (Ted Knight)
2. **Carl Spackler** (Bill Murray)
3. **Al Czervik** (Rodney Dangerfield)
4. **Maggie O'Hooligan** (Sarah Holcomb)
5. **The Bishop** (Henry Wilcoxon)

"License to kill gophers—by the government of the United Nations."

The Brat Pack vs. The Rat Pack Five-on-Five Celebrity Basketball Game

If you want a working definition of the Brat Pack, please buy our first book, *Who Can It Be Now?* On page 33, you'll find an incredibly accurate description of our Brat Pack friends. But for now, why don't we partake in a little fantasy B-ball?

Coach: John Hughes vs. Sam Giancana

John Hughes, whose use of the Triangle Offense makes him one of the premier strategists in all of basketball, is a genius when it comes to positional play ("Judd, you moron, the camera is over here!"). Sam Giancana, on the other hand, calls all the shots. Now that the Kennedy assassination hoopla is behind him, watch for "Momo" and his boys to take it to the Brat Pack's throats.

EDGE: Rat Pack

Molly Ringwald vs. Sammy Davis Jr.

The redheaded actress can post up easily against the diminutive Davis, creating a nice little mismatch, but she's a little slow off the dribble. The fleet-footed, thinly mustachioed Sammy D. is a whiz at handling the ball and can tap-dance around most defensive opponents.

EDGE: Even

Emilio Estevez vs. Joey Bishop

Estevez, who has played a jock, a coach, and a garbage man in his featured roles, is a solid two-guard who can also play point and small forward. Joey, while a cut above most of Vegas's degenerates, is one of the weaker links on this potent Rat Pack team.

EDGE: Brat Pack

Ally Sheedy vs. Peter Lawford

Ally hasn't shown us much the last few years. Her below-average rebounding and limited defensive ability mean her days as a starting player in this league are over. Lawford's off-the-court woes mirror those of his famous brother-in-law, but this former CBA-er lacks the vision on the court and the overall skills that made JFK the Washington Bullets' most lethal weapon.

EDGE: Even

Anthony Michael Hall vs. Dean Martin

Hall has had some trouble adjusting to the power forward position. Although he added muscle to his frame, he hasn't shown the ability to shake the wimpy reputation that has shadowed him throughout his career. Dean, a twelfth-year man out of UNLV, is a solid shot blocker with all the intangibles who'll do whatever it takes to win. Don't be fooled by this guy's noncompetitive demeanor: He'll throw a few elbows to dominate the inside game.

EDGE: Rat Pack

Judd Nelson vs. Frank Sinatra

Once a promising phenom, the chunky Nelson looks to be going the way of Sam Bowie and Chris Washburn. Despite his annoying presence in the paint, at his age it's going to be difficult to develop new skills. Fully recovered from an ACL injury that nearly wiped out his '97 season, Sinatra is once again a portrait of consistency. He's coach Giancana's go-to guy in every situation. Ol' Blue Eyes is worth every penny of his sky-high salary.

EDGE: Rat Pack

Brat Pack vs. Rat Pack Bunch

Rob Lowe	Don Rickles
Andrew McCarthy	Jerry Lewis
Robert Downey Jr.	Shirley MacLaine
Demi Moore	Lauren Bacall

EDGE: Brat Pack

1. "I'm getting input here that I'm reading as relatively hostile."
2. "Drunk definitely—I don't know if you could call it driving."
3. "Do you think I'd speak for you? I don't even know your language."
4. "Love is an illusion."
5. "I don't know why you're both so worried. So I bop him for a couple of years."
6. "I'm obsessed, thank you very much."
7. "I loathe the bus. There has to be a more dignified mode of transportation."
8. "Jesus. Do I look like I'm ready for homework?"
9. "I don't screw to get respect. That's the difference between you and me."

1. **The Geek/Farmer Ted** (Anthony Michael Hall) in *Sixteen Candles*
2. **Billy** (Rob Lowe) in *St. Elmo's Fire*
3. **John Bender** (Judd Nelson) in *The Breakfast Club*
4. **Kevin** (Andrew McCarthy) in *St. Elmo's Fire*
5. **Jules** (Demi Moore) in *St. Elmo's Fire*
6. **Kirby** (Emilio Estevez) in *St. Elmo's Fire*
7. **Samantha** (Molly Ringwald) in *Sixteen Candles*
8. **Julian Wells** (Robert Downey Jr.) in *Less Than Zero*
9. **Allison Reynolds** (Ally Sheedy) in *The Breakfast Club*

"Now put your clothes back on, and I'll
buy you an ice cream."

There were five Bond movies made in the '80s and, sadly, *Moonraker* wasn't one of them. But we still have to praise Richard Kiel's brilliant performance as the menacing Jaws in that film, and mention what a blatant *Star Wars* knockoff the whole thing was.

James Bond (Roger Moore, this time around) says the line on the preceding page in 1981's ***For Your Eyes Only***, the most notable Bond film of the decade for a couple of reasons. It is notable to serious Bond lovers for being the first Bond movie to be based on an Ian Fleming short story instead of a novel. And it is notable to prurient people because Tula Cossey, who plays one of the women hanging out by the pool, used to be a man.

Times Square to Tinseltown: Broadway Goes Hollywood

Whenever Neil Simon so much as sneezed in the '80s, someone from Hollywood wanted to turn that bodily function into a movie script. Riding the crest of Simon's '60s and '70s popularity, Hollywood adapted a whopping total of four Neil Simon plays (five if you count television's *Plaza Suite*). We've listed a few of them below, along with some other Broadway or off-Broadway originals that found their way onto the big screen. And if you can name one movie that Aileen Quinn was in—besides *Annie*—our publisher will FedEx you two free tickets to see Broadway's version of *Footloose*. (Just kidding.)

1. "Do you think that we could find a place where we can meet, not in silence and not in sound?"

2. "I didn't really like most of those guys then, but today I love every damn one of them. Life is weird, you know."

3. "If I had a nose like Florine, I wouldn't go around saying 'Merry Christmas' to anybody."

4. "You ain't never gonna be no more than you are right now: a chicken-shit sheriff in a chicken-shit town!"

5. "I have just seen the golden palace of the Himalayas. Puberty is over. Onwards and upwards."

6. "Why any kid would want to be an orphan is beyond me."

7. "Come here, Norman. Hurry up. The loons. The loons! They're welcoming us back."

8. "Mediocrities everywhere, I absolve you. I absolve you. I absolve you. I absolve you. I absolve you all."

1. **James Leeds** (William Hurt) in *Children of a Lesser God*
2. **Eugene** (Matthew Broderick) in *Biloxi Blues*
3. **Daisy Werthan** (Jessica Tandy) in *Driving Miss Daisy*
4. **Miss Mona Stangley** (Dolly Parton) in *The Best Little Whorehouse in Texas*
5. **Eugene** (Jonathan Silverman) in *Brighton Beach Memoirs*
6. **Miss Hannigan** (Carol Burnett) in *Annie*[*]
7. **Ethel Thayer** (Katharine Hepburn) in *On Golden Pond*
8. **Antonio Salieri** (F. Murray Abraham) in *Amadeus*

[*]Incidentally, Aileen Quinn, who was spectacular in her role as Annie, made only two other movies in the '80s. If you've seen *Ozu no mahôtsukai* (the Japanese version of *The Wizard of Oz*) or *The Frog Prince*, then you've probably already seen *Footloose* on Broadway and on video about a zillion times.

"I am not an animal. I am a human being."

Yeah, right. Basically, if Rocky Dennis married Dumbo's sister . . . Okay, so we won't go that route again, but you have to admit that it would be quite a beauty contest if Rocky from *Mask* and **John Merrick** (John Hurt, see the photo on page 82), the Elephant Man, had a pose-down onstage. Directed by David Lynch—another guy who'd fit right in at a ten-in-one show—and starring a pre–Hannibal "the Cannibal" Anthony Hopkins, ***The Elephant Man*** garnered praise in critical circles (especially among the carny crowd) and earned eight Academy Award nominations. Although it didn't win any of the awards, it is rumored that David Lynch accurately guessed the weights of each one of that year's winners.

From Gygax to Gump—Tom Hanks in the '80s

Long before he was winning Best Actor every year for playing a character with one malady or another, Tom Hanks was a pretty successful comedic actor. Instead of playing serious leading men like Andrew Beckett in *Philadelphia*, he was playing goofy leading men like Allen Bauer in *Splash*. Of course, before his movie career, Hanks was a TV star. Everyone remembers him from *Bosom Buddies*. But far cooler than that was his role as Robbie in *Mazes and Monsters*, the Dungeons & Dragons–based TV movie that also starred Murray Hamilton (who was brilliant in *The Graduate* and *Jaws*) and Chris Makepeace (who was brilliant in *Meatballs* and *My Bodyguard*).

1. "I'm fine. I was looking forward to a nice quiet cup of coffee, but now I'm awake."
2. "Nobody knocks off an old man in my neighborhood and gets away with it."
3. "Okay, but I get to be on top."
4. "Do you have any idea what falls into an industrial sausage press, including rodent hairs and bug excrement?"
5. "Little problem in the kitchen."
6. "No, I don't remember, Paula. You got me drunk."
7. "I think I put in the hours, don't you?"
8. "Attention, passengers, we are now leaving 'nun central' on our journey to Hell and beyond."
9. "All my life I've been waiting for someone, and when I find her she's a fish."

1. **Scott Turner** in *Turner & Hooch*
2. **Ray Peterson** in *The 'Burbs*
3. **Josh Baskin** in *Big*
4. **Pep Streebeck** in *Dragnet*
5. **Walter Fielding** in *The Money Pit*
6. **Richard** in *The Man with One Red Shoe*
7. **Lawrence Bourne III** in *Volunteers*
8. **Rick Gassko** in *Bachelor Party*
9. **Allen Bauer** in *Splash*

 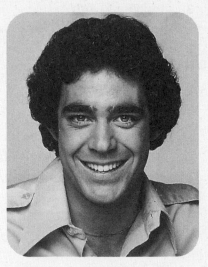

Separated at birth?

Christmastime in Hollywood

Even though *A Christmas Story* is by far the best Christmas movie of the '80s (and one of the best of all time), there were quite a few Christmas-themed movies to hit the big screen in that decade. In this section, we've listed a bunch of movies that are filled with holiday mirth and cheer. We've even included one horror flick to really get you in the Yuletide spirit (and one war movie that just has *Christmas* in the title). And while the horror flick doesn't quite measure up to *It's a Wonderful Life*, as the producers promise: It's guaranteed to "sleigh" you. Ho. Ho. Ho.

1. "Clark, stop it. I don't want to spend the holidays dead."

2. "Be sure to drink your Ovaltine. Ovaltine? A crummy commercial? Son of a bitch!"

3. "No, you are a hallucination brought on by alcohol—Russian vodka, poisoned by Chernobyl."

4. "But if you're bad, then your name goes in the Bad Boys and Girls book."

5. "God, I wish they'd stop hitting me."

1. **Ellen Griswold** (Beverly D'Angelo) in *National Lampoon's Christmas Vacation*
2. **Ralphie** (Peter Billingsley) in *A Christmas Story*
3. **Frank Cross** (Bill Murray) in *Scrooged*
4. **Harry Stadling** (Brandon Maggart) in *You Better Watch Out*
5. **Colonel John Lawrence** (Tom Conti) in *Merry Christmas, Mr. Lawrence*

"Listen, mate. You could have declined this mission. You didn't have to serve under me, right?"

"War. What is it good for? Absolutely nothing."

Unless, of course, you're Mel Gibson and two of your early movies were Peter Weir's well-regarded *Gallipoli* and the underrated Aussie war flick ***Attack Force Z.*** *Attack Force Z* was always one of our favorites. The plot revolves around Gibson—as **Captain P. G. Kelly**—and Sam Neill as World War II commandos who rescue survivors of a plane crash on a Japanese-held island. Pete fondly remembers one happy Tuesday back in 1983 when he feigned illness to stay home from school because HBO was showing *Victory*, *Attack Force Z*, and *Clash of the Titans* back-to-back-to-back!

"I've been out with a lot of girls at this school. I don't see what makes you so different."

While bad boy Billy Zabka was glomming all of the evil-jock roles in several high profile '80s movies, pretty boy James Spader was being cast as the quintessential preppy villain. Spader's character **Steff** in John Hughes's *Pretty in Pink* rivals Zabka's character Johnny in *The Karate Kid* as the best teen-movie nemesis of the decade. Apparently 1987 was a busy year for both Spader and Zabka, so when John Hughes cast the antagonist in *Some Kind of Wonderful*, he got stuck with Craig Sheffer.

All Mixed Up, Part III

1. "Never trust a junkie."
2. "Hilda is dead, and here's something to note. You can't bury her at sea, 'cause her bosoms will float."
3. "I'm not an actor. I'm a movie star."
4. "Life rarely gives us what we want at the moment we consider appropriate."
5. "The purpose of our suffering is only more suffering."
6. "There's nothing more inconvenient than an old queen with a head cold."
7. "Tell me the first thing that pops in your head."
8. "Master, I've had enough aggravation for one day."
9. "If you get her pregnant, I'll blow your dick off."
10. "I never wanted to use macramé to kill."
11. "You know what they say about slugs. They always leave slime in their tracks."
12. "You know—you kind of remind me of a bull terrier of some kind."
13. "Isn't love great, Chris? One minute you're a god, the next minute you're a scum-sucking pig."
14. "You were born with an asshole, Doris, you don't need Chuck."
15. "Red light stop, green light go, yellow light go very fast."
16. "I'd make a great Gordon, Gordon."
17. "Do you have a name? Do you have a police record? Where are you from?"
18. "No ex-husband of Gloria's ever has to apologize to me about anything."

1. **Nancy Spungen** (Chloe Webb) in *Sid and Nancy*
2. **Dr. Tart** (Tim Conway) in *The Private Eyes*
3. **Alan Swann** (Peter O'Toole) in *My Favorite Year*
4. **Mrs. Moore** (Peggy Ashcroft) in *A Passage to India*
5. **Eddie Jessup** (William Hurt) in *Altered States*
6. **Carroll Todd** (Robert Preston) in *Victor/Victoria*
7. **Dave** (Gene Wilder) in *See No Evil, Hear No Evil*
8. **Radu** (John Byner) in *Transylvania 6-5000*
9. **Lou Fimple** (Fred Ward) in *Secret Admirer*
10. **Lu-Lu Fishpaw** (Mary Garlington) in *Polyester*
11. **Louis Cyphre** (Robert De Niro) in *Angel Heart*
12. **Dr. Jeff Cooper** (Sam Shepard) in *Baby Boom*
13. **Richard "Stick" Montgomery** (Aidan Quinn) in *Stakeout*
14. **Samantha Belmont** (Kelli Maroney) in *Night of the Comet*
15. **Starman** (Jeff Bridges) in *Starman*
16. **Mac MacIntyre** (Peter Riegert) in *Local Hero*
17. **Interrogation Sergeant** (Armin Shimerman) in *The Hitcher*
18. **Ivan Travalian** (Al Pacino) in *Author! Author!*

"I love my dead gay son!"

137

You either love *Heathers* or you hate it. Starring Timothy Leary's god-daughter, Winona Ryder, this dark teen comedy tried very hard to satirize high school life in the late '80s. It succeeds when it shows Winona, Shannen Doherty, and a bunch of other hotties parading around the halls in miniskirts. It fails anytime annoying Jack Nicholson–wannabe Christian Slater appears on-screen. Doherty, who plays one of the three Heathers, used this role to cut her teeth as Hollywood's favorite bad girl and effectively set the template for every other role she'd ever play, including Brenda on *Beverly Hills, 90210* (opposite James Dean–wannabe Luke Perry) and Prue on *Charmed* (opposite Luke Perry–wannabe T. W. King).

We, however, like to remember Doherty's career in the early '90s, when she regularly infuriated everyone she worked with, posed nude in *Playboy* more often than Charo appeared on *The Love Boat*, and was ordered by the State of California to undergo anger-management counseling for smashing a beer bottle on some guy's car window. Oh yeah, the line is spoken by **Kurt's Dad** (Mark Carlton) at the funeral of his "dead gay son."

At the end of his life, when Steven Spielberg looks back at his career, he might not want to think too hard about the '80s. Sure, he had some incredible successes. But we're still not sure if even the wildly popular *E.T.* and the amazing *Raiders of the Lost Ark* make up for all the crap that Steve lent his name to as "executive producer." *The Goonies*? One of the seminal film directors of our time was responsible for greenlighting *The Goonies*? Hard to believe. And that's not even the worst of it. But don't worry, in this section you won't find any lines from **batteries not included*, *The Money Pit*, or anything else that Spielberg solely produced.

1. "Young women no good these days. Got their legs open for every Tom, Dick, and Harpo."
2. "I can't be with a guy that looks like I won him in a raffle."
3. "You can't do this to me, I'm an *American*!"
4. "I learned a new word today. Atom bomb."
5. "Nazis. I hate these guys."
6. "How do you explain school to a higher intelligence?"
7. "Fortune and glory, kid. Fortune and glory."

1. **Albert Johnson** (Danny Glover) in *The Color Purple*
2. **Dorinda Durston** (Holly Hunter) in *Always*
3. **Marion** (Karen Allen) in *Raiders of the Lost Ark*
4. **Jim** (Christian Bale) in *Empire of the Sun*
5. **Indiana Jones** (Harrison Ford) in *Indiana Jones and the Last Crusade*
6. **Elliott** (Henry Thomas) in *E.T. The Extra-Terrestrial*
7. **Indiana Jones** (Harrison Ford) in *Indiana Jones and the Temple of Doom*

"I'll have what she's having."

Wasn't that scene in **_When Harry Met Sally . . ._** where Meg Ryan fakes an orgasm in Katz's Deli really great?

No way. There is absolutely nothing funny about a woman faking an orgasm. Nothing. But apparently, every woman in America thought it was the funniest scene ever, and because of it, _When Harry Met Sally . . ._ became one of the most popular movies of 1989. Billy Crystal transformed himself from Fernando ("You look mahvelous") to the guy who hosted the Oscars before Whoopi Goldberg. Meg Ryan was crowned the cutest girl in America. Bruno Kirby remained Bruno Kirby. And of course, director Rob Reiner's mom, Estelle—who played the **Older Woman Customer** at Katz's—just wanted to have whatever Sally was having.

Ain't That a Shane?

Let's face it, the '80s weren't exactly the golden era of Westerns. *Young Guns* was not *Shane*, director Christopher Cain was not George Stevens, and Emilio Estevez, Kiefer Sutherland, Lou Diamond Phillips, and Charlie Sheen couldn't hold Alan Ladd's spittoon. But the '80s did have a few memorable Westerns, even if they did leave you hollering at the end, "Shane, Shane, come back!"

(Okay, so we cheated a little here: Two of the movies listed below are actually comedies with western motifs and another one is a drama that has the word *cowboy* in the title. We were going to include 1983's *Triumphs of a Man Called Horse*, but we didn't want anyone to get the wrong idea.)

1. "Blind Pete always said you'd hang. I guess tomorrow at dawn he'll be proved right."
2. "Nothing like a good piece of hickory!"
3. "Can you two-step?"
4. "Give me a tall glass of warm gin with a human hair in it."
5. "Male company will be a pleasant relief in this hothouse of female emotions."
6. "See, you got three or four good pals, why then, you got yourself a tribe. There ain't nothing stronger than that."
7. "I like these guys. They are funny guys. Only kill one of them."

1. **Emmett** (Scott Glenn) in *Silverado*
2. **The Preacher** (Clint Eastwood) in *Pale Rider*
3. **Sissy** (Debra Winger) in *Urban Cowboy*
4. **Rex O'Herlihan** (Tom Berenger) in *Rustlers' Rhapsody*
5. **Rosemary** (Lorraine Bayly) in *The Man from Snowy River*
6. **William H. Bonney/Billy the Kid** (Emilio Estevez) in *Young Guns*
7. **El Guapo** (Alfonso Arau) in *¡Three Amigos!*

There aren't enough adjectives in the dictionary to heap all the praise on George Lucas that he deserves. The *Star Wars* trilogy pretty much assures him of God status for all eternity. Although Irvin Kershner and Richard Marquand are the nominal directors of *The Empire Strikes Back* and *Return of the Jedi* respectively, the creative relationship between Lucas and his directors was kind of like the relationship Señor Wences had with his irrepressible hand puppet—Lucas was responsible for every frame in both films. *Empire* in some ways is the high point of the trilogy. *Jedi* has its moments, but it'd be a lot better if you could just cut all the crap with the Ewoks. Rumor has it that Endor was originally supposed to be populated with Wookiees, but we figure the merchandising folks saw more possibilities in hooded little teddy bears than in a bunch of Chewbacca clones. The Ewoks weren't Lucas's only '80s mistake, however. He was, after all, responsible for the cinematic turd that was *Howard the Duck*.

Darth Vader was so cool it took three actors to play him: James Earl Jones did his voice, David Prowse was the guy in the suit, and Sebastian Shaw was the face when Vader's mask came off.

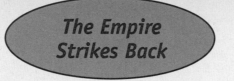

The Empire Strikes Back

1. "Laugh it up, fuzzball!"
2. "Sir, the possibility of successfully navigating an asteroid field is approximately 3,720 to 1!"
3. "You must unlearn what you have learned."
4. "I am altering the deal. Pray I don't alter it any further."
5. "He's no good to me dead."

1. **Han Solo** (Harrison Ford)
2. **C-3PO** (Anthony Daniels)
3. **Yoda** (Frank Oz)
4. **Darth Vader** (James Earl Jones)
5. **Boba Fett** (Jeremy Bulloch)

(Insert Chewbacca sound here.)

The *Star Wars* Matching Game

Well, you might have been able to get all the quotes from *The Empire Strikes Back*, but can you match the actor who either played or voiced these unforgettable *Empire Strikes Back* and *Return of the Jedi* creatures?

1. C-3PO

2. R2-D2

3. Boba Fett

4. Chewbacca

5. Yoda

6. Admiral Ackbar

7. Sy Snootles

8. Bib Fortuna

9. Wicket

10. Lobot

a. Peter Mayhew

b. John Hollis

c. Michael Carter

d. Kenny Baker

e. Annie Arbogast

f. Warwick Davis

g. Jeremy Bulloch

h. Anthony Daniels

i. Tim Rose

j. Frank Oz

1. **h**
2. **d**
3. **g**
4. **a**
5. **j**
6. **i**
7. **e**
8. **c**
9. **f**
10. **b**

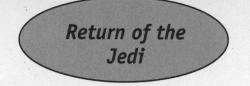

Return of the Jedi

1. "The Emperor is not as forgiving as I am."
2. "Your overconfidence is your weakness."
3. "You have a power I don't understand and could never have."
4. "Everything that has transpired has done so according to my design."
5. "Luke, you're going to find that many of the truths we cling to depend greatly on our own point of view."

1. **Darth Vader** (James Earl Jones)
2. **Luke Skywalker** (Mark Hamill)
3. **Princess Leia Organa** (Carrie Fisher)
4. **Emperor Palpatine** (Ian McDiarmid)
5. **Obi-Wan Kenobi** (Sir Alec Guinness)

"I hate Illinois Nazis."

Jake (John Belushi) and Elwood are two of the most memorable characters of the decade, and ***The Blues Brothers*** ranks as one of the most quotable movies of all time. Anyone with half a brain would have left the Blues Brothers legacy alone when John Belushi died in 1982. But who said anyone in Hollywood had half a brain? In 1998, Dan Aykroyd and cowriter John Landis went back to the well to put together *Blues Brothers 2000*. We would rather watch Aykroyd in that stupid *Coneheads* movie than see him do the blues shtick without his funnier half.

Deities of the '80s—Kim Basinger

All right, so '80s sex goddess Kim Basinger hasn't made the best decisions in her life. As if marrying Alec Baldwin wasn't bad enough, Kim went off to buy her own town, Braselton, in her home state of Georgia. We can forgive the Alec Baldwin thing (her role in *Nine ½ Weeks* makes up for that), but who the hell buys their own town? Who does she think she is? Marlon Brando? How did she fight the temptation to rename Braselton Basingerburg? We just don't get it. Her being from Athens, Georgia, though, might explain some of her bizarreness. After all, that's the town R.E.M. is from, and everyone knows how much of a freak Michael Stipe is.

1. "I mean, let's face it. You're not exactly normal, are you?"
2. "Will you tell me the composition of your radar beam or not?"
3. "Here's your chance to run for it—your very last chance."
4. "Whenever I see you, you're always smiling at me."
5. "Baseball. Max was right, you know. You're . . . you're just a mystery."
6. "I'll have a double Bloody Mary with plenty of Worcestershire sauce."

1. **Vicki Vale** in *Batman*
2. **Celeste Martin** in *My Stepmother Is an Alien*
3. **Nadia Gates** in *Blind Date*
4. **Elizabeth** in *Nine ½ Weeks*
5. **Memo Paris** in *The Natural*
6. **Domino Petachi** in *Never Say Never Again*

"A hundred million terrorists in the world
and I gotta kill one with feet smaller
than my sister."

Full of gratuitous violence, one-liners, and nonstop action, *Die Hard* was ripped off by nearly every action movie of the '90s. This line, spoken by **John McClane**, was just one of the many that helped turn former bartender Bruce Willis into a superstar.

The man who played David Addison (opposite Cybill Shepherd) in *Moonlighting* was ubiquitous in the late '80s. Remember those annoying Seagram's Golden Wine Cooler ads he sang in opposite Sharon Stone? Some music exec must have liked what he heard, and Willis made the most of the opportunity: His weak blues number, "Respect Yourself," went all the way up to Number Five in 1987.

Lights, Camera, Action Jackson!

After he wrote the kick-ass "Theme from *Shaft*" and before he was known to adolescents as the voice of Chef on *South Park*, Isaac Hayes played the Duke of New York in John Carpenter's classic *Escape from New York*. The thing about these '80s action movies is that there's usually just one star, trained in one martial art or another, fighting off a slew of bad guys and winning the love of a good woman all at the same time. But *Escape from New York* was different; it harkened back to the great action movies of years before and featured a brilliant ensemble cast including Lee Van Cleef, Donald Pleasence, Ernest Borgnine, Harry Dean Stanton, and, of course, Kurt Russell as the futuristic antihero whose name you'll find below.

1. "You break my record, now I break you, like I break your friend."
2. "Do you believe in Jesus?"
3. "What does this have to do with military intelligence?"
4. "You're the disease, and I'm the cure."
5. "Call me Snake."
6. "Excuse me, I have to go. Somewhere there is a crime happening."
7. "Yippee-ki-yay, motherf**ker."
8. "When I want your opinion, I'll beat it out of you."
9. "I ain't got time to bleed."

1. **Chong Li** (Bolo Yeung) in *Bloodsport*
2. **Paul Kersey** (Charles Bronson) in *Death Wish II*
3. **Nico Tuscani** (Steven Seagal) in *Above the Law*
4. **Marion Cobretti** (Sylvester Stallone) in *Cobra*
5. **Snake Plissken** (Kurt Russell) in *Escape from New York*
6. **Murphy/RoboCop** (Peter Weller) in *RoboCop*
7. **John McClane** (Bruce Willis) in *Die Hard*
8. **Eddie Cusack** (Chuck Norris) in *Code of Silence*
9. **Blain** (Jesse "the Body" Ventura) in *Predator*

"No wire hangers . . . *ever!*"

Someone on the Razzie committee either loves **Joan Crawford** or hates Faye Dunaway, because there's just no way in hell ***Mommie Dearest*** deserved to win Worst Picture, Worst Screenplay, Worst Actress, Worst Supporting Actor, and Worst Supporting Actress of 1982. To add salt to the wound, *Mommie Dearest* even won the Razzie for Worst Picture of the Decade in 1990. The movie lost out to unwatchable offal like *Leonard Part 6* and *Howard the Duck*. Who votes for this stuff anyway? Big-time Crawford buff, Taco?

Now listen up, Taco. Joan Crawford is certainly A-OK in our book. But what child wasn't traumatized by the immortal "wire hanger" scene when Joan gets medieval on poor little Christina Crawford's ass? Perhaps Christina should have heeded Joan's earlier advice to studio executives: "Don't f**k with me fellas. This ain't my first time at the rodeo." Now who in their right mind would razz her?

Remakes

It's easy to sit back and complain that Hollywood is out of ideas. Just look at all the bad TV shows that get turned into movies. Another way the folks out in La La land demonstrate their lack of creativity is through all the unnecessary remakes that are produced each year. Why in God's name would you bother to remake *Psycho*, *Sabrina*, or even *Cape Fear**?

There are many notable examples of '80s remakes and you'll find lines from them below. It's interesting to note that the novel *Brewster's Millions* had actually already been adapted for film a stunning six times *before* Walter Hill's 1985 version, which starred Richard Pryor, John Candy, and Jerry Orbach. Despite all that talent, the seventh trip to the well was so bad that nobody's tried to remake *Brewster's Millions* again since.

1. "Be afraid. Be very afraid."
2. "Gentlemen, do you think I'm a lowlife?"
3. "This is life. Here. Now. Take it or leave it."
4. "Subject in transit has changed his shoes. Riding a bicycle—ten-speed, I suspect."
5. "I'm no longer a carnivore. I don't eat anything that's ever had parents."

[*Sorry, Marty.]

1. **"Ronnie" Quaife** (Geena Davis) in *The Fly*
2. **Montgomery Brewster** (Richard Pryor) in *Brewster's Millions*
3. **Sydney Fuller** (Meg Ryan) in *D.O.A.*
4. **Reese** (Tom Noonan) in *The Man with One Red Shoe* (remake of *The Tall Blond Man with One Black Shoe*)
5. **Nicole Hollis** (Demi Moore) in *Blame It on Rio* (remake of *One Wild Moment*)

To B or Not to B: The B Movie Matching Game

B movie fanatics of the world unite! Who needs *Sixteen Candles* or *St. Elmo's Fire* when you can have *Hollywood Chainsaw Hookers* and *Killer Klowns from Outer Space*? We would have given you lines from these cinematic tours de force, but our publisher couldn't have paid us enough to sit through *Hell Comes to Frogtown* again. Seeing it in 1987 when it was first released and again in 1995 as part of the Rowdy Roddy Piper Film Festival in Winnipeg was certainly enough. So instead, we present to you the B movie match game. Can you match the brilliant B movie with its even more brilliant director?

1. **Chopper Chicks in Zombietown**

2. **Crazy Fat Ethel II**

3. **Hollywood Chainsaw Hookers**

4. **Killer Klowns from Outer Space**

5. **Microwave Massacre**

6. **Redneck Zombies**

7. **Sorority Babes in the Slimeball Bowl-O-Rama**

8. **Zombie Nightmare**

9. **Space Mutiny**

10. **Alien from L.A.**

a. Fred Olen Ray

b. Wayne Berwick

c. Nick Phillips

d. David DeCoteau

e. Albert Pyun

f. Stephen Chiodo

g. Jack Bravman

h. David Winters

i. Dan Hoskins

j. Pericles Lewnes

165

1. i
2. c
3. a
4. f
5. b
6. j
7. d
8. g
9. h
10. e

"We've got bush."

Well, the incredibly vile, offensive, eructating Dudley Dawson, aka **Booger**, wasn't talking about the '80s folkie who sang "Running Up That Hill" here. He was talking about you know what, in one of the great sophomoric hits of the decade, *Revenge of the Nerds*. Starring the venerable Robert Carradine, Timothy Busfield, and Curtis Armstrong—as Lewis, Poindexter, and Booger—the Nerds movie fit the most basic movie paradigm of David triumphing over Goliath. But it still took a grand total of *four* guys to write it.

Of course, everyone knows that Anthony Edwards (Gilbert) went on to *ER* fame, so let's take a look at what a few of the other male *ER* cast members were doing back in the day:

1. George Clooney appeared in the sitcom *E/R*—which also starred Elliott Gould and Jason Alexander—and *Return of the Killer Tomatoes!*
2. Eriq LaSalle played Eddie Murphy's Jheri-curled foil in *Coming to America*.
3. Gedde Watanabe was the cartoonish exchange student, Long Duk Dong, in *Sixteen Candles*.
4. Noah Wyle was collecting baseball cards of Brian Downing, Juan Beniquez, Rob Wilfong, and Donnie Moore out in California.

Deities of the '80s—Harrison Ford

Few movie stars are as universally well liked as Harrison Ford. Have you ever met anybody who doesn't like this guy? He starred in three of the four highest-grossing films in the '80s, and he's great in every one of them. His success has continued on to the point where producers have to promise him their firstborn sons just to get him to read a script. But to hear Harrison Ford in an interview, all he wants to do is fly planes and hang out on his ranch in Wyoming—a righteous dude all the way around. Interestingly, of all the movies Ford has worked on over the past three decades, you'll never guess which one is his favorite. Hint: There's a quote from it on this page.

1. "I didn't know how long we'd have together. Who does?"
2. "How do I look? I mean, do I look Amish?"
3. "If what you want isn't washed up on this beach, you probably don't need it."
4. "You're the first woman I've seen at one of these damn things that dresses like a woman."
5. "Oldies, I like oldies."
6. "I told you—don't call me Junior."
7. "Well, why don't you use your divine influence and get us out of this?"
8. "Nothing shocks me. I'm a scientist."
9. "I thought they smelled bad on the outside."
10. "It's not the years, honey—it's the mileage."

1. **Deckard** in *Blade Runner*

2. **John Book** in *Witness*

3. **Allie Fox** in *The Mosquito Coast* *

4. **Jack Trainer** in *Working Girl*

5. **Richard Walker** in *Frantic*

6. **Indiana Jones** in *Indiana Jones and the Last Crusade*

7. **Han Solo** in *Return of the Jedi*

8. **Indiana Jones** in *Indiana Jones and the Temple of Doom*

9. **Han Solo** in *The Empire Strikes Back*

10. **Indiana Jones** in *Raiders of the Lost Ark*

[*Harrison's favorite movie.]

Okay, so we've already used a few lines from these movies in the book. But in our opinion the Indiana Jones trilogy still deserves more. Did you know that Indiana Jones was the name of George Lucas's dog? And did you ever notice any of the weird *Star Wars* references in *Raiders of the Lost Ark*? If you look carefully at Jock's plane registration number right after the opening sequence, you'll see that it's OB-CPO. OB for Obi-Wan and CPO for C-3PO. And in the Well of Souls scene, if you examine the hieroglyphics carefully, you can see engravings of both R2-D2 and C-3PO on a post to the right of Indy and Sallah.

1. "So once again, Jones, what was briefly yours is now mine."
2. "It tells me that goose-stepping morons like yourself should try reading books instead of burning them."
3. "I hate the water, and I hate getting wet, and I hate you."
4. "Asps. Very dangerous. You go first."
5. "And this is how we say good-bye in Germany."

1. **Belloq** (Paul Freeman) in *Raiders of the Lost Ark*
2. **Henry Jones** (Sean Connery) in *Indiana Jones and the Last Crusade*
3. **Willie Scott** (Kate Capshaw) in *Indiana Jones and the Temple of Doom*
4. **Sallah** (John Rhys-Davies) in *Raiders of the Lost Ark*
5. **Vogel** (Michael Byrne) in *Indiana Jones and the Last Crusade*

"The Master Control Program has chosen
you to serve your system on the
game grid."

To be fair, it might take you several minutes to remember that this line is spoken by David Warner as **Sark** (back when that name meant a computer-generated bad guy, not the writer lady who implores us all to live our rich, succulent lives to the fullest—with full-color illustrations!). But any fan of '80s sci-fi could tell you that the preceding line is from *Tron*—the movie in which a hacker (Jeff Bridges) is sucked into a video game and forced to dethrone the evil Master Control Program and replace it with the human-friendly Tron. Tron was played brilliantly by underrated genius Bruce Boxleitner (who played Scarecrow in the runaway TV hit *Scarecrow and Mrs. King* as well as many other challenging roles over the past three decades).

Tron was one of the first movies to use computer-generated special effects and has quite a cult following to this day. It also set an '80s box-office record for Most Income Generated from Ten-Year-Olds' Birthday Parties by a Movie Not Starring Harrison Ford.

All Mixed Up, Part IV

1. "Just like a wop to bring a knife to a gunfight."
2. "Excuse me, we're from Noisebusters. Do you know where the Menudo concert is?"
3. "If this is foreplay, I'm a dead man."
4. "Beware of the moors."
5. "You can't drown, you fool. You're immortal."
6. "God, does it always shrivel up like that when you shower?"
7. "The army couldn't afford drapes? I'll be up at the crack of dawn here."
8. "Watches are a confidence trick invented by the Swiss."
9. "My name is a killing word."
10. "I don't trust happiness. I never did and I never will."
11. "Uncle Sam don't give a shit about your problems."
12. "This is the Cosby decade. America loves black people."
13. "You should have seen the Atlantic Ocean in those days."
14. "If we're not back by morning, call the President."
15. "Why are women so uptight?"
16. "To whom, Brother. To whom, Brother."
17. "Put me back in! Put me back in!"

1. **James Malone** (Sean Connery) in *The Untouchables*
2. **Danny Costanzo** (Billy Crystal) in *Running Scared*
3. **Jack Bonner** (Steve Guttenberg) in *Cocoon*
4. **David Kessler** (David Naughton) in *An American Werewolf in London*
5. **Ramirez** (Sean Connery) in *Highlander*
6. **Ramona** (Cathy Moriarty) in *Neighbors*
7. **Judy Benjamin** (Goldie Hawn) in *Private Benjamin*
8. **Chiun** (Joel Grey) in *Remo Williams: The Adventure Begins . . .*
9. **Paul Atreides** (Kyle MacLachlan) in *Dune*
10. **Mac Sledge** (Robert Duvall) in *Tender Mercies*
11. **Richard Chance** (William L. Petersen) in *To Live and Die in L.A.*
12. **Mark Watson** (C. Thomas Howell) in *Soul Man*
13. **Lou** (Burt Lancaster) in *Atlantic City*
14. **Jack Burton** (Kurt Russell) in *Big Trouble in Little China*
15. **Dell** (Gary Busey) in *D.C. Cab*
16. **Caesar** (Malcolm Danare) in *Heaven Help Us*
17. **Mikey** (Bruce Willis) in *Look Who's Talking*

"I have come here to chew bubblegum
and kick ass, and I'm all out of
bubblegum."

When he wasn't busy losing 75 percent of his hearing in his infamous dog-collar match with Greg "the Hammer" Valentine, professional wrestler and Canada (not Scotland) native Rowdy Roddy Piper was making movies. His most memorable role came as **Nada** in John Carpenter's not-so-classic *They Live.* The movie, however, is redeemed by two things that Piper does (using much the same creativity he brought to Piper's Pit week after week). One is the ad-libbed line on the preceding page. The other is what may well be the longest fistfight in all of '80s cinema (sorry, Sly). Piper and actor Keith David were supposed to throw a couple of punches at each other but decided to slug it out for real over the course of about an hour. Carpenter, probably eager for the movie's running time to exceed ninety minutes, left the whole thing in.

Sports—Not the Huey Lewis Album

What do you think about when you think of sports in the '80s? The arrogance and excellence of the '86 Mets? The Islanders' amazing run of four Stanley Cups in a row?[*] Phil Simms's nearly perfect performance in the 1986 Super Bowl against the Broncos? Steve Zungul and Shep Messing leading the Arrows to yet another MISL title? The heated rivalry between Sunday Silence and Easy Goer? Well, if you were a big movie fan in the '80s, it's more likely that you'll remember Robert Redford as Roy Hobbs literally knocking the cover off the ball or Gene Hackman as Coach Norman Dale freaking out on the sideline during the state championships.

1. "I thought everybody in Indiana played basketball."
2. "If you build it, he will come."
3. "I guess some mistakes you never stop paying for."
4. "There's never been a ballplayer slept with me who didn't have the best year of his career."
5. "The American Express Card—don't steal home without it."
6. "When I run, I feel his pleasure."
7. "You don't kick well, you don't dribble well, but you could be a good goalkeeper."
8. "I guess we all do unexpected things sometimes, don't we?"
9. "Wanna go, pretty boy?"

[*]For the record, Frank is a Rangers fan.

1. **Coach Norman Dale** (Gene Hackman) in *Hoosiers*
2. **"Shoeless" Joe Jackson** (Ray Liotta) in *Field of Dreams*
3. **Roy Hobbs** (Robert Redford) in *The Natural*
4. **Annie Savoy** (Susan Sarandon) in *Bull Durham*
5. **Willie Mays Hayes** (Wesley Snipes) in *Major League*
6. **Eric Liddell** (Ian Charleson) in *Chariots of Fire*
7. **Luis Fernandez** (Edson Arantes do Nascimento aka Pelé) in *Victory*
8. **Brian Kelly** (Christian Slater) in *Gleaming the Cube*
9. **Racki** (George Finn) in *Youngblood*

"Amazing tradition—they throw a great party for you on the one day they know you can't come."

Okay, so seven college friends from the '60s get back together in the '80s, having traded in their radical ideas for careers working for the Man. This movie was better the first time we saw it, when it was called *The Return of the Secaucus Seven* and directed by John Sayles. But the rest of America didn't seem to mind as much, since **The Big Chill**— riding the strength of a soon-to-be all-star cast (Tom Berenger, Glenn Close, William Hurt, Kevin Kline)—and its classic soundtrack became huge hits despite the pilfered concept and fatuous script. Maybe that sounds a tad harsh, but we expected more from the guy who wrote the screenplays for *Raiders of the Lost Ark* and *The Empire Strikes Back*. This line was spoken by **Michael,** who was played by the ever-versatile muscid, Jeff Goldblum.

Those who sat through *The Postman* will appreciate the movie's opening sequence, where Kevin Costner appears as a corpse.

Before John Grisham[*] came along with his incredibly inventive titles—*The Client*, *The Partner*, *The Firm*—'80s screenwriters perfected their own version of the legal thriller. Granted, they didn't use titles as clever as Mr. Grisham's. But they did stretch the bounds of creativity to come up with some startlingly creative gems of their own, like *The Accused*, *The Verdict*, and *Suspect*.

1. "I heard someone screaming and it was me."
2. "There is nothing in the world that will make me go back to criminal work."
3. "A wonderful thing—a subpoena."
4. "Your Honor, with all due respect, if you're going to try my case for me, I wish you wouldn't lose it."
5. "I spend all of my day with murderers and rapists."

[*]Incidentally, we hope John Grisham gets on his knees and thanks the Lord every night, for if Scott Turow hadn't paved the way with his 1987 best-selling novel, *Presumed Innocent*, Grisham would still be practicing law in a farmhouse in Oxford, Mississippi.

1. **Sarah Tobias** (Jodie Foster) in *The Accused*
2. **Teddy Barnes** (Glenn Close) in *Jagged Edge*
3. **James Wells** (Wilford Brimley) in *Absence of Malice*
4. **Frank Galvin** (Paul Newman) in *The Verdict*
5. **Kathleen Riley** (Cher) in *Suspect*

"Two dollars!"

Whatever happened to Savage Steve Holland? The visionary director, once described as John Hughes if John Hughes had been dropped on his head as a baby, seems to have fallen off the face of the earth. Can you imagine if Shakespeare had written *Hamlet*, then two inferior knock-offs, then disappeared for fifteen years only to reemerge as the writer/director of *Love Boat: The Movie*? Well that's what happened to Savage Steve. Sort of.

This line is spoken by **Johnny** (Demian Slade) to Lane Myer in ***Better Off Dead***, the first and by far the best of Savage Steve's efforts. He rounded out what has come to be known as the Savage Steve trilogy with *One Crazy Summer*, which featured the not-so-clever pairing of John Cusack and Bobcat Goldthwait, and *How I Got Into College*, which starred Corey Parker, who was not only an ersatz Cusack, but also an ersatz Corey.*

[*The link between all three of Savage Steve's movies is Curtis Armstrong (aka Booger from the *Revenge of the Nerds* oeuvre and aka Herbert Viola from *Moonlighting*). So, don't be surprised if he has a cameo as Charo's date in the new *Love Boat*.]

Nanoo Nanoo— Robin Williams in the '80s

Pop quiz:

How do you know which Robin Williams is going to show up on the big screen in the '90s? Will it be the quiet, pensive teacher who encouraged adolescent boys to seize the day as John Keating, or the goofy, exuberant alien who bedeviled audiences as Mork?[*] It's easy: Just check the movie poster to see if Williams is sporting facial hair. Of course, Williams's movie career got started in the '80s after *Happy Days* spin-off *Mork & Mindy* became a huge hit and Robert Altman decided to cast him as a spinach-eating sailor man.

1. "O Captain! My Captain!"

2. "I've got tides to regulate, comets to direct. I don't have time for flatulence and orgasms."

3. "Put these on and say 'There's no place like home, there's no place like home,' and you can be there."

4. "Yes, in America anything is possible. Good-bye for now, beloved family."

5. "What kind of man gives cigarettes to trees?"

6. "We are civilized people and civilized people obey rules, you neolithic dipshit."

7. "I want spinach, I'll ask ya for spinach."

[*]Fans will find it interesting that Williams's first serious role was as Tommy Wilhelm in Saul Bellow's *Seize the Day*.

1. **John Keating** in *Dead Poets Society*
2. **King of the Moon** in *The Adventures of Baron Munchausen*
3. **Adrian Cronauer** in *Good Morning, Vietnam*
4. **Vladimir Ivanoff** in *Moscow on the Hudson*
5. **Donald Quinelle** in *The Survivors*
6. **Garp** in *The World According to Garp*
7. **Popeye** in *Popeye*

"You don't seem to want to accept who you are dealing with. You are dealing with a man who is an expert—with guns, with knives, with his bare hands."

You'd think with all the money Sly Stallone made from *Rocky*, he'd take some speech lessons. You'd also think that if he was going to start doing some non-action movies, he'd take some acting lessons, too. But who are we to surmise? At least **First Blood** was an action movie and Stallone didn't have to speak too much in his role as the deranged Vietnam vet John Rambo. Based on the book by David Morrell, *First Blood* also starred Richard Crenna and Brian Dennehy. Crenna, as **Colonel Troutman**, tries to convince a very stubborn, egotistical Dennehy, who plays Sheriff Teasle, that Rambo is a man who's been "trained to ignore pain, to ignore weather—to live off the land and eat things that would make a billy goat puke." By the time *Rambo III* came out in 1988, a lot of audiences were ready to do the same.

Pete's favorite Brian Dennehy moment: When he realized that the man onstage in Broadway's 1999 revival of *Death of a Salesman* was the same guy who did the Zantac heartburn medicine commercials.

Frank's favorite Brian Dennehy moment: When he realized that the man doing the Zantac heartburn medicine commercials was the same guy who told his high school theater company that they had virtually no shot at successful acting careers.

And Now for Something Completely Different: Monty Python in the '80s

Asking which Monty Pythonite is your favorite is kind of like asking what the air speed velocity of an unladen swallow is. It's a downright difficult question and you might get killed if you answer incorrectly in certain circles. Nevertheless, the '80s were a pretty ripe time for everyone involved in the British comedy troupe and for good reason: The Python crew did not rest on their *Holy Grail* and *Life of Brian* laurels. Instead, they wrote, directed, and starred in a bunch of critically acclaimed movies that also rank among our personal favorites. And if you don't think the dearly departed Graham Chapman was the best of the bunch, then your mother was a hamster and your father smelled of elderberries.

1. "Four foot one? Well, that . . . that . . . that . . . that . . . is a long time, isn't it? Jolly good."
2. "Otto tried to k-k-kiss me."
3. "Better get a bucket. I'm gonna throw up."
4. "The wrong man was delivered to me as the right man."
5. "We're actors, not figments of your imagination. Now get a grip."

1. **Robin Hood** (John Cleese) in *Time Bandits*
2. **Ken** (Michael Palin) in *A Fish Called Wanda*
3. **Mr. Creosote** (Terry Jones) in *Monty Python's The Meaning of Life*
4. **Jack Lint** (Michael Palin) in *Brazil*
5. **Desmond** (Eric Idle) in *The Adventures of Baron Munchausen*

"You're a suburban white punk
just like me."

Mike Nesmith certainly has had an interesting life, hasn't he? How cool would it be if *your* mom had invented Liquid Paper? Of course, Nesmith was also by far the most talented member of the Monkees—though we suppose that gets back to the old nicest guy in prison routine. It was disappointing that he didn't join Peter Tork, Davy Jones, and Mickey Dolenz when the reunited Monkees played Westbury Music Fair in 1986 (a show we were both at, by the way). But in the '80s, Nesmith was busy producing movies and TV shows. One of them was Alex Cox's cult-classic ***Repo Man***, which features this line from **Otto** (Emilio Estevez).

The Hellion

Okay, he's not a deity of the '80s in any sense, but nonetheless the multitalented Crispin Hellion Glover is a memorable figure to emerge from '80s movies. Ever see this guy on Letterman ("I'm a strong man, Dave")? He nearly beheaded the talk-show host with a karate kick. Ever hear about Glover's birthday? He celebrates it twice a year, on April 20 and September 20. Ever hear about his hobbies? He apparently collects dolls' eyes and has a wine bottle with three mouse embryos inside. Believe it or not, in the '90s, Glover may have gone even more off the rails. Between acting gigs, he's spent his time recording spoken word albums; rewriting obscure, out-of-print nineteenth-century tomes; and directing the first film to star children with Down's syndrome.[*]

1. "He thinks that's funny. He thinks that's a funny thing he's doing."
2. "I poked at it with a stick."
3. "Have you tried to score with her yet?"
4. "Stories. Science fiction stories."
5. "Eddie, ya gotta get me a piece."

[*]Our favorite Glover book, *Rat Catching: Studies in the Art of Rat Catching,* was published in 1987.

1. **Jimmy** in *Friday the 13th—The Final Chapter*
2. **Layne** in *River's Edge*
3. **Jack** in *My Tutor*
4. **George McFly** in *Back to the Future*
5. **Danny** in *Teachers*

"The academy is taking all kinds today.
Anybody can get in. Even you."

The new police recruits. Call them slobs. Call them jerks. Just don't call them when you're in trouble.[*]

So here's a question for you: What happens when you cast a bad comedian whose shtick is making incredibly stupid noises, a hot actress who made a career starring in horribly bad '80s movies, and Steve Guttenberg? You get the first of a whole slew of pathetically bad **Police Academy** movies. It's hard to imagine that Steve Guttenberg, whose mug appears in about seven hundred photos in the Pizza Cove Pizzeria near Plainedge High School (his alma mater) on Long Island, lasted for three of the six sequels. It's easy to see why David Graf (who played Tackleberry) and Michael Winslow (who played Larvell Jones) stuck around for all seven movies—what else did they have to do? But Steve Guttenberg sticking around for four is preposterous. Even Kim Cattrall, whose lack of prejudice landed her roles in the likes of *Porky's*, *Mannequin*, and *Honeymoon Academy*, had enough sense to split after the first one. This line was spoken by **Captain Reed** (Ted Ross) to the perpetual wiseacre, Carey Mahoney (Guttenberg).

[*]We wish we could take credit for such poetry, but we have to admit that this was the actual tag line used on the *Police Academy* poster.

198

Proctor! The *Police Academy* Matching Game

Here are the names of the six *Police Academy* sequels. Can you match the number with the name? We're not going to include the two *Police Academy* television spinoffs here. You know, the animated version that came out in 1988 and the series (starring Michael Winslow!) that came out in 1997.

a. *City Under Siege*

b. *Citizens on Patrol*

1. **Police Academy 2 (1985)**

c. *Mission to Moscow*

2. **Police Academy 3 (1986)**

d. *Back in Training*

3. **Police Academy 4 (1987)**

e. *Their First Assignment*

4. **Police Academy 5 (1988)**

f. *Assignment: Miami Beach*

5. **Police Academy 6 (1989)**

6. **Police Academy 7 (1994)**

1. **e**
2. **d**
3. **b**
4. **f**
5. **a**
6. **c**

"Don't ever lose your sense of humor, Dan. Don't *ever* lose your sense of humor."

Pretentious fans of David Mamet's *Sexual Perversity in Chicago* will tell you that **About Last Night . . .** is a complete piece of trash. Certain John Belushi fans will say the same thing about his younger brother. They both couldn't be further from the truth. Granted, the love story between Rob Lowe and Demi Moore in *About Last Night . . .* is typically boring Hollywood tripe, complete with a waterlogged Rob Lowe professing his undying fealty to a love-scarred Demi Moore in a Chicago rainstorm. And Jim Belushi *is* responsible for starring in the likes of *K-9* and *Homer & Eddie*. But his great comedic performance as **Bernie Litco** makes what could have been a very boring movie actually very funny. Thankfully, every sex scene in the movie is between Rob Lowe and Demi Moore, so you don't have to worry about seeing Jim Belushi and Elizabeth Perkins naked.

Deities of the '80s—Sigourney Weaver

One cool thing about Sigourney Weaver is that in 1989 she was up for two Academy Awards for two different movies. She was up for Best Actress for *Gorillas in the Mist* and Best Supporting Actress for *Working Girl*. She didn't win either, but any girl who changes her name from Susan to Sigourney after reading *The Great Gatsby* gets our vote anytime. The five-foot-eleven-inch Weaver made her big-screen debut as Alvy Singer's (Woody Allen) date in *Annie Hall* and broke out two years later as Lieutenant Ellen Ripley in *Alien*. Her family's solid Hollywood pedigree (her father was president of NBC and her mother was an actress) got Weaver started, but her strong, aggressive female roles propelled her to stardom. At the wrap party for *Ghostbusters*, Sigourney read from a poem she wrote about the movie. Fitzgerald she is not, but the opening stanza went like this: "I am a little Ghostbuster/Sigourney is my name/This picture cost a lot of bread/Let's hope it makes the same."

1. "Okay, but after dinner, I don't want you putting any of your old cheap moves on me."
2. "They're not going to turn this mountain into a goddamn zoo."
3. "I've cleared the month of June, and I am, after all, me."
4. "I say we take off and nuke the entire site from orbit. That's the only way to be sure."
5. "Are you the Keymaster?"
6. "If the PKI take over, they'll slaughter every European in Jakarta."
7. "That's the only people they know."

1. **Dana Barrett** in *Ghostbusters II*
2. **Dian Fossey** in *Gorillas in the Mist*
3. **Katherine Parker** in *Working Girl*
4. **Ellen Ripley** in *Aliens*
5. **The Gatekeeper/Dana Barrett** in *Ghostbusters*
6. **Jill Bryant** in *The Year of Living Dangerously*
7. **Tony Sokolow** in *Eyewitness*

"From hell's heart, I stab at thee. For hate's sake, I spit my last breath at thee."

Now that line should be familiar to everybody for a couple of reasons, or at least familiar to anyone who was an English major. But since there wasn't an adaptation of Herman Melville's *Moby Dick* done in the '80s, there's only one right answer: These words are spoken by **Khan** in ***Star Trek II: The Wrath of Khan***. The part was played brilliantly by Ricardo Montalban, who had a few weeks off from his role as Mr. Roarke on *Fantasy Island*. *The Wrath of Khan,* a sequel to the classic "Space Seed" episode of *Star Trek*, ranks as the finest moment for the crew of the *Enterprise*.*

"Do I smell fajitas?"

*There's actually a mathematical formula that can tell you if the *Star Trek* movie you're thinking of renting is worth the three bucks. If you can divide the sequel's number evenly by two, it's a go. If not, you might as well be watching *Lost in Space* reruns.

Bad Sequel, VIII

Don't get us wrong. We've got nothing against someone trying to make a quick buck. But what happened with movie sequels in the '80s was ridiculous. *Jaws* (one of our favorite movies of all time) is a perfect example. 1978's *Jaws 2* was bad enough—and at least that had Roy Scheider in it. But then the '80s brought us Louis Gossett Jr. and Dennis Quaid hamming it up in the 3-D extravaganza creatively named *Jaws 3-D*. Let's face it: The special effects in the *Creature from the Black Lagoon* they showed on Channel 11 (with the special red and blue glasses you got from Burger King) were just as good. But *Jaws 3-D* is a classic compared to *Jaws: The Revenge*, in which they dug up Lorraine Gary (to reprise her role as Ellen Brody), and enlisted Michael Caine ("It's a *shawk!*") and Mario Van Peebles (Sonny Spoon) to help catch the fearsome great white. *Jaws* kept anyone who saw it from ever wanting to go to the beach again. *Jaws: The Revenge* kept anyone who saw it from ever wanting to go to the movies again.

1. "Why don't you be the ball? If I wanted to be a piece of sports equipment, I'd be a ladies bicycle seat."
2. "But I don't blame them, 'cause one time I turned into a dog and they helped me."
3. "Besides, there's gotta be more to life than making out."
4. "For man with no forgiveness in heart, life worse punishment than death."
5. "Hey loverboy, give me a hand. Your wish has just come true."
6. "Look at the size of that Russian!"
7. "Norman was not convicted of murder. He was found not guilty by reasons of insanity."

1. **Jack** (Jackie Mason) in *Caddyshack II*
2. **Louis Tully** (Rick Moranis) in *Ghostbusters II*
3. **Stephanie** (Michelle Pfeiffer) in *Grease 2*
4. **Mr. Miyagi** (Pat Morita) in *The Karate Kid, Part II*
5. **Roxy** (Sally Kellerman) in *Meatballs III*
6. **Warner Wolf** as himself (Commentator no. 2) in *Rocky IV*
7. **Dr. Raymond** (Robert Loggia) in *Psycho II*

"If we can't be great, then there's no sense in ever playing music again, Sal."

If you didn't get this quote, don't fret. Here are a few hints to help you figure it out: John Cafferty and the Beaver Brown Band, "On the Dark Side," Tom Berenger, Ellen Barkin, and the guy who played Eddie Moscone in *Midnight Run*. Well, if you don't know it by now, you never will. The movie is **Eddie and the Cruisers** and the line is spoken by Michael Paré, who plays the enigmatic rock star **Eddie Wilson**. The movie spawned a couple of Top 40 hits, but by the decade's end, no one cared a lick about Michael Paré or John Cafferty. And though *Eddie and the Cruisers II* was released in 1989 (with both Paré and Cafferty attached), the movie's subtitle, *Eddie Lives!*, sounded more like a horror movie featuring Iron Maiden's mascot than the sequel to an early '80s cult hit.

"Theme from . . ."
and Countless
Other Hit Songs
from Movies,
Part II

1. "I'd like to glue a *Playboy* centerfold inside every one of Reverend Moore's hymnals."
2. "Just leave with me. There's no reason for you to stay—not here, not in L.A."
3. "When I was in fourth grade, I stole my uncle Joseph's toupee and glued it to my face."
4. "I wanna be just like you. I figure all I need is a lobotomy and some tights."
5. "There are several quintessential moments in a man's life: losing his virginity, getting married, becoming a father, and having the right girl smile at you."
6. "I feel the need—the need for speed."
7. "You could have killed him, couldn't you?"
8. "Wait a minute, Doc—are you telling me you built a time machine out of a De Lorean?"
9. "They know about the rat poison. I might as well just turn myself in."
10. "Everyone who drinks is not a poet. Some of us drink because we're not poets."

1. **Ren** (Kevin Bacon) in ***Footloose*** ("Footloose" by Kenny Loggins or "Let's Hear It for the Boy" by Deniece Williams)

2. **Clay** (Andrew McCarthy) in ***Less Than Zero*** ("Going Back to Cali" by L. L. Cool J)

3. **Lawrence "Chunk" Cohen** (Jeff Cohen) in ***The Goonies*** ("The Goonies 'R' Good Enough" by Cyndi Lauper)

4. **John Bender** (Judd Nelson) in ***The Breakfast Club*** ("Don't You [Forget About Me]" by Simple Minds)

5. **Kirby** (Emilio Estevez) in ***St. Elmo's Fire*** ("St. Elmo's Fire [Man in Motion]" by John Parr)

6. **Pete "Maverick" Mitchell** (Tom Cruise) in ***Top Gun*** ("Take My Breath Away" by Berlin)

7. **Daniel** (Ralph Macchio) in ***The Karate Kid, Part II*** ("Glory of Love" by Peter Cetera)

8. **Marty McFly** (Michael J. Fox) in ***Back to the Future*** ("The Power of Love" by Huey Lewis and the News)

9. **Violet** (Lily Tomlin) in ***9 to 5*** ("9 to 5" by Dolly Parton)

10. **Arthur Bach** (Dudley Moore) in ***Arthur*** ("Arthur's Theme [The Best That You Can Do]" by Christopher Cross)

"You don't like hangers? It's hangers that clothe you and hangers that feed you."

It's merely stating the obvious to say that Richard Dreyfuss wasn't nearly as cool in the '80s as he was in the '70s. And to be fair, anybody who was in both *American Graffiti* and *Jaws* couldn't be expected to go anywhere but down. Still, Dreyfuss's drop was fairly precipitous—like Dickie Thon after the Mike Torrez fastball. It's not so much that his movies were that bad—we liked *Tin Men*, and *Stakeout* has its moments (even though Emilio Estevez can't carry Robert Shaw's fishing rod). Dreyfuss's well-publicized drug problems metamorphosed him from the charming young guy who won an Oscar in *The Goodbye Girl* to the gray-haired curmudgeon who played Jay Trotter in *Let It Ride* and **Dave Whiteman** in ***Down and Out in Beverly Hills***.*

*Yes, we know that a decade had elapsed in between, but c'mon, in the '80s Dreyfuss looked forty-two going on sixty.

Woody Allen isn't the first guy you think of when you talk about '80s movies. But in truth, when he wasn't playing the clarinet at Michael's Pub on Monday nights, he was writing some of the funniest lines of the decade. A busy guy with a guilty conscience, Woody worked constantly—all in all he directed ten and a third films in the '80s (the third being *New York Stories*). Two films you won't find lines from below are his dramas *September* and *Another Woman*. Perhaps that's because we believe Woody's films should reflect the perspective of a funny, neurotic guy from Brooklyn, not that of the father of Scandinavian cinema.

1. "Only art you can control. Art and masturbation. Two areas in which I am an absolute expert."

2. "When are you gonna grow up? You're like one of those creatures in Greek mythology who's half goat."

3. "I never delivered a baby before, and I just thought that ice tongs were the way to do it."

4. "It's very important to be guilty. I'm guilty all the time, and I never did anything."

5. "Great. That means I'll have to see the Ice Capades again."

6. "I never forgot that New Year's Eve when Aunt Bea awakened me to watch 1944 come in."

7. "What is the guy so upset about? He's not the first person to be compared to Mussolini."

1. **Sandy Bates** in *Stardust Memories*
2. **Andrew** in *A Midsummer Night's Sex Comedy*
3. **Zelig** in *Zelig*
4. **Danny Rose** in *Broadway Danny Rose*
5. **Mickey** in *Hannah and Her Sisters*
6. **The Narrator** in *Radio Days*
7. **Cliff Stern** in *Crimes and Misdemeanors*

"The band gets first shot at any extra money, right, Melissa? The brass section could really use the bucks."

Okay, if you know this quote, then you are either an '80s movie fanatic or friends with one of the cast members. In our case, we're both. ***Catch Me If You Can*** is a typical '80s PG movie, complete with a typical high school setting and characters with names like "Quarterback," "Stoner," "(Grease) Monkey," "Drama Kid," and "The Frosh." The first film by writer/director Stephen Sommers, *Catch Me If You Can* starred Matt Lattanzi, who was once married to Olivia Newton-John. While it also features M. Emmet Walsh, who played Dr. Dolan in *Fletch* and Coach Turnbull in *Back to School*, this movie is significant for other reasons, the most important of which is that it gives *us* a "Kevin Bacon" number of four. The quote on the preceding page was spoken by **Band Kid**, played by Robert Kempe, who helped with the research for this book. So, to put things in proper perspective, here's our link to the Six Degree Man. Thanks, Robert.

Robert Kempe was in
Catch Me If You Can

with M. Emmet Walsh,
who was in *Wildcats*

with Bruce McGill, who
was in *Animal House*

with . . . Kevin Bacon

You think Steve Martin knows how Lou Reed feels? Despite all the excellent stuff both men have done in their careers, they're both tormented by one song from the past. In Reed's case it's "Walk on the Wild Side." In Martin's, it's "King Tut." But both men have managed to get on with their lives nicely. In Steve's case, he just took the arrow out of his head and became a movie star. The banjo player/author/stand-up/actor who went gray even earlier than Bob Baffert had a great run of successful movies in the '80s, including our favorite, *¡Three Amigos!* All the amigos were great, but their thunder was stolen by one of the decade's most menacing film villains, El Guapo (played by Alfonso Arau). "Would you say I have a plethora of piñatas?"

1. "Women have choices and men have responsibilities."
2. "It is better to be truthful and good than to not."
3. "You're like one of those Chatty Cathy dolls except I'm not pulling the string, you are."
4. "I want to look like Diana Ross."
5. "I thrill when I drill a bicuspid."
6. "Great! You killed the invisible swordsman."
7. "We don't have to have sex, there's plenty other things we can do."
8. "Just because my grandfather didn't rape the environment and exploit the workers doesn't make me a peasant."
9. "You! You're the elevator killer. Merv Griffin!"
10. "My plan was to kiss her with every lip on my face."

1. **Gil** in *Parenthood*
2. **Freddy Benson** in *Dirty Rotten Scoundrels*
3. **Neal Page** in *Planes, Trains & Automobiles*
4. **Charlie C. D. Bales** in *Roxanne*
5. **Orin Scrivello, D.D.S.** in *Little Shop of Horrors*
6. **Lucky Day** in *¡Three Amigos!*
7. **Larry Hubbard** in *The Lonely Guy*
8. **Roger Cobb** in *All of Me*
9. **Dr. Michael Hfuhruhurr** in *The Man with Two Brains*
10. **Rigby Reardon** in *Dead Men Don't Wear Plaid*

"Merry Christmas. The shitter was full."

As funny as the *National Lampoon Vacation* movies are, they wouldn't be nearly as good if it wasn't for the hilarious antics of Clark W. Griswold's (Chevy Chase) crass, inbred, white-trash brother-in-law, **Eddie** (Randy Quaid). Eddie, who is a staple in each one of the *Vacation* movies, really shines in ***Christmas Vacation*** when he shows up in his sewage-infested recreational vehicle to crash the Griswold family Christmas.

Written by the inimitable John Hughes, the *Vacation* movies entertained moviegoers for a decade with their hilarious depictions of a typical nuclear family. It all began in 1983 when Clark nearly imploded on the way to Wally World and it ended in 1989 with Clark almost setting his house on fire during the Christmas holiday season. In case you were wondering, we're not even recognizing 1997's *Vegas Vacation* as a movie.

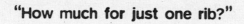

"How much for just one rib?"

This line was spoken by a not-yet-famous Chris Rock as **Rib Joint Customer** in Keenen Ivory Wayans's hilarious send-up of the blaxploitation genre, *I'm Gonna Git You Sucka*.

This movie featured the best casting of the decade, bringing together the stars of classics like *Shaft*, *Cleopatra Jones*, *Foxy Brown*, *Three the Hard Way*, and *Cornbread, Earl and Me*. They even threw in Willona from *Good Times* and the guy with the best name ever—Clu Gulager—just for good measure. If only they could have gotten Pam Grier, Fred "the Hammer" Williamson, and somebody from *Superfly* (we're listening to Curtis Mayfield's amazing soundtrack as we write this), the coup would have been complete.

Corey Feldman and Corey Haim

by Louise

Emilio and Charlie move over! These Coreys are so hot! We here at *Teen-Tiger* hear that the Coreys love long walks on the beach! And they're really into the environment! Wearing wool is definitely out: Corey F. is allergic! Ladies looking to land a Corey must avoid smoking and swearing and must be prepared to endure '90s substance-abuse programs and career lapses including straight-to-video strikeouts like *Meatballs 4* and *Snowboard Academy*.

1. "I should be at the dance. I was at the dance—dancing perfectly with a hot chick."
2. "Les, to live in fear is not to live at all."
3. "My own brother, a goddamn shit-sucking vampire. You wait till Mom finds out."
4. "I guess everybody has their own idea of fun. Some people go to football games, other people do less *superficial* things."
5. "Hey, Mikey, gotta go to the bathroom?"
6. "Hey lame-o, get out of my yard!"
7. "By the time we get there, the kid won't even be dead anymore."
8. "Can we slow down a little? The party's going to go on all night."
9. "One, two, three, four, five new ones. Now can I have one?"

1. **Dinger** (Corey Haim) in *Dream a Little Dream*
2. **Dean** (Corey Feldman) in *License to Drive*
3. **Sam** (Corey Haim) in *The Lost Boys*
4. **Lucas** (Corey Haim) in *Lucas*
5. **Clarke "Mouth" Devereux** (Corey Feldman) in *The Goonies*
6. **Ricky Butler** (Corey Feldman) in *The 'Burbs*
7. **Teddy Duchamp** (Corey Feldman) in *Stand by Me*
8. **Tommy** (Corey Feldman) in *Friday the 13th: The Final Chapter*
9. **Pete** (Corey Feldman) in *Gremlins*

"Lighten up, Francis."

Sergeant Hulka's (Warren Oates) pithy response to Psycho's (George Jenesky) "Any of you homos touch me, and I'll kill you" speech in *Stripes* became the catchphrase for 1981 teens everywhere. Starring Bill Murray and Harold Ramis—the former *SCTV* star and the genius behind the classic puerile comedies *Animal House*, *Meatballs*, and *Caddyshack*, to name a few—*Stripes* featured an ensemble cast that included John Candy (Ox), John Larroquette (Captain Stillman), Judge Reinhold (Elmo), and a youthful Sean Young (Louise, in only her second feature film). The antics of Murray et al. were so funny they made *Private Benjamin* look like *Back to Bataan*. So if you're wondering if *Stripes* is among our favorite comedies of the decade . . . "That's the fact, Jack!"

The Horror! The Horror!

Remember the "Thriller" video, where Michael slips a ring on his "girlfriend's" finger, cooing "It's official" before turning into some sort of supernatural were-puma? Well, the spoof video, directed by John Landis, turned out to be the most-watched horror movie of the decade. Whether you were an actual fan of this horror genre or just wanted an excuse to cop a quick feel from your terrified girlfriend, you'll appreciate the eleven lines below.

1. "Don't expect it to tango; it has a broken back."
2. "We can't bury Sharyn. She's our friend."
3. "You want me to salute that pile of walking pus? Salute my ass!"
4. "We're friends till the end, remember?"
5. "You can try to kill me, Dan. But you can't. You can only make me dead."
6. "I will show you things that you have never seen and I will see the life run out of you."
7. "Come here, damn you. I want to touch you."
8. "Silver bullets or fire—that's the only way to get rid of the damn things. They're worse than cockaroaches."
9. "Goddamn you, woman. Goddamn you."
10. "I'm a U.S. citizen. Think about that."
11. "I do have a way with these creatures."

1. **Herbert West** (Jeffrey Combs) in *Re-Animator*
2. **Ashley J. "Ash" Williams** (Bruce Campbell) in *The Evil Dead*
3. **Rhodes** (Joseph Pilato) in *Day of the Dead*
4. **Chucky** (Brad Dourif) in *Child's Play*
5. **Dobbs** (Jack Albertson) in *Dead and Buried*
6. **Eva/Alma** (Alice Krige) in *Ghost Story*
7. **Frank** (Sean Chapman) in *Hellraiser*
8. **Bookstore Owner** (Dick Miller) in *The Howling*
9. **Ed Harley** (Lance Henriksen) in *Pumpkinhead*
10. **Dennis** (Bill Pullman) in *The Serpent and the Rainbow*
11. **Paul Ruth** (Patrick McGoohan) in *Scanners*

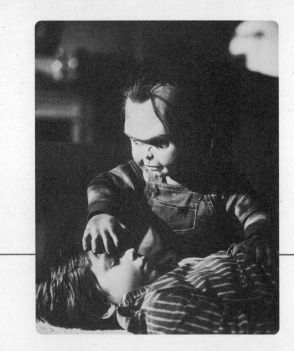

I Want Candy— John Candy in the '80s

This is the kind of guy John Candy was: On March 3, 1994, on the set of *Wagons East*—an abominably bad '90s movie—Candy cooked his assistants a pot of pasta before retiring to bed. He died in his sleep. Now that's our kind of movie star. Do you think Drew Carey even knows how to turn on an oven? Do you think Drew Carey even knows what an oven is? He knows what pasta is, that much is obvious. But would he cook his assistants a meal? We wonder. Candy, on the other hand, was always viewed as a gentle soul. Everybody knows the giant actor was a member of the talented *SCTV* group. But did you know that he had a cameo in Ray Parker Jr.'s "Ghostbusters" video?

1. "I am Djour Djilios."
2. "I don't have a college degree. I don't even have a job."
3. "Nature all around us, boys. Take it in. Take it all in."
4. "We'd have more luck playing pickup sticks with our butt cheeks than we will getting a flight out of here before daybreak."
5. "It's not that we're afraid—far from it. It's just that death, it just isn't us."
6. "Yeah, it's a fifty caliber. They used to use it to hunt buffalo with. Up close. It's only legal in two states. This isn't one of them."
7. "You see, drinking is really a matter of algebraic ratios."
8. "I'm gonna walk out of here a lean, mean, fightin' machine."
9. "Who wants an Orange Whip? Orange Whip? Orange Whip? Three Orange Whips."

1. **Harry Crumb** in *Who's Harry Crumb?*
2. **Buck Russell** in *Uncle Buck*
3. **Chet** in *The Great Outdoors*
4. **Del Griffith** in *Planes, Trains & Automobiles*
5. **Barf** in *Spaceballs*
6. **Frank Dooley** in *Armed and Dangerous*
7. **Freddie Bauer** in *Splash*
8. **Ox** in *Stripes*
9. **Burton Mercer** in *The Blues Brothers*

"May the Schwartz be with you."

Sensitive *Star Wars* fans would probably smite us with a battery-operated Kenner plastic light saber if they knew **Spaceballs** was one of our favorite spoofs of the decade. But that shouldn't come as a surprise, since Mel Brooks is responsible for some of the funniest movies ever made. With Rick Moranis as the evil Dark Helmet, Bill Pullman as the renegade hero Lone Starr, and Mel Brooks as the diminutive borscht-belt comedian cum sage **Yogurt**, *Spaceballs* mimicked the great *Star Wars* trilogy in every way.* Right down to the shocking revelation that Dark Helmet was really Lone Starr's "father's brother's nephew's cousin's former roommate."

*The movie also featured brilliant performances by John Candy, the Chewbacca-like Barf; Joan Rivers, the C-3PO-ish Dot Matrix; and Daphne Zuniga as the beautiful Princess Vespa.

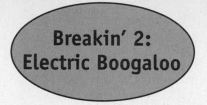

Breakin' 2: Electric Boogaloo

These days, all you need is a sample from a Sister Sledge tune and your picture in *People* magazine and the studios are sure to come knocking at your door. But back in the day, rappers did rap movies and not bad Hollywood summer thrillers like *Independence Day*. Can you match these fresh rappers with the movies they appeared in?

a. *Breakin'*

b. *Krush Groove*

1. **Fab Five Freddy**   c. *Tougher Than Leather*

2. **The Fat Boys**   d. *Wild Style*

3. **Doug E. Fresh**   e. *Beat Street*

4. **Ice-T**   f. *Disorderlies*

5. **Kurtis Blow**

6. **Run-D.M.C.**

1. **d**
2. **f**
3. **e**
4. **a**
5. **b**
6. **c**

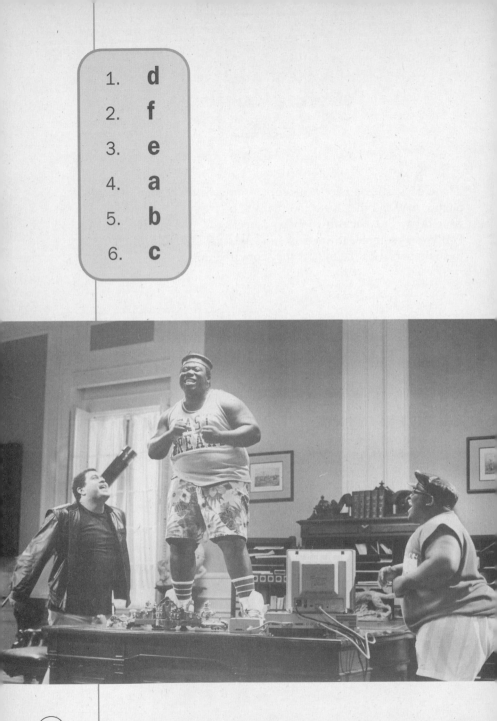

"Inconceivable!"

We were going to give you "Hello. My name is Inigo Montoya. You killed my father. Prepare to die," but that would have taken the fun out of guessing the character's name. Instead, we chose this gem of a quote lisped quite emphatically throughout **The Princess Bride** by **Vizzini**, who is played by the great Wallace Shawn. Other great men to star in this movie? Christopher Guest and André the Giant. It's interesting to note that costar Billy Crystal must have become enamored with André the Giant's gargantuan size, because in the '90s, everyone's favorite Oscar host paired up with another seven footer (inept basketball player Gheorghe Muresan) to film the box office disaster *My Giant*. The conclusion to be drawn here: Moviegoers appreciate midgets (the Munchkins, the Seven Dwarfs, the Oompa Loompas) and are frightened by gigantic foreign freaks (unless they're professional wrestlers).

Deities of the '80s—Glenn Close

Any actress who signs on to play a character who kills and cooks a pet rabbit is a deity in our book. Our one complaint about that incredibly famous scene from *Fatal Attraction*: That it wasn't Eddie Rabbitt boiling in that vat of scalding liquid instead of just the Gallagher family's pet *lapin*—just kidding, we love Eddie Rabbitt! Close's role as the sociopath Alex (who goes from wearing all white to all black as the movie progresses) was actually turned down by other '80s stars Barbara Hershey and Debra Winger. It turned out to be a much-talked-about role, and Close's performance earned her one of five Oscar nominations in the '80s. And while she's still considered an excellent actress, her last Academy Award nomination came at the end of the decade, in 1989, for her role in *Dangerous Liaisons*.

1. "In the end I distilled everything to one wonderfully simple principle: Win or die."
2. "Well, bring the dog. I love animals. I'm a perfect cook."
3. "Did your mother ever wash your mouth out with soap and water?"
4. "I used to look for you in crowds thinking someday maybe you'd be there. Somewhere I stopped."
5. "Did you have to be in such a good mood?"
6. "The doctor says he'll be fine once they take the stitches out of his tongue and unwire his jaw."

1. **Marquise de Merteuil** in *Dangerous Liaisons*
2. **Alex Forrest** in *Fatal Attraction*
3. **Teddy Barnes** in *Jagged Edge*
4. **Iris** in *The Natural*
5. **Sarah** in *The Big Chill*
6. **Jenny Fields** in *The World According to Garp*

"Marriage is a concept invented by people who were lucky to make it to twenty without being eaten by dinosaurs. Marriage is extinct."

This quote is from **St. Elmo's Fire** and it is spoken by **Kevin**, the character played by babyfaced '80s mainstay Andrew McCarthy. But what can we possibly say about *St. Elmo's Fire* that hasn't already been said by '80s movie fanatics everywhere? Nothing. And that is why we're going to talk about *Weekend at Bernie's*, the pièce de résistance of '80s cinema. Starring the aforementioned McCarthy, *Weekend at Bernie's* has all the trappings of greatness: two virile young men, an idyllic island retreat, and an actor whose portrayal of a dead man is fit for the London stage. Its place in the pantheon of the world's greatest films is by all means secure.

Super Heroes, Super Freaks

*Look. It's a bird. It's a plane. It's ...
Richard Pryor in* Superman III. There
are some things that just shouldn't be al-
lowed, and casting Richard Pryor in an
abominably bad Superman sequel is one of them.
But that isn't the most interesting thing about the Man of
Steel movies. Did you know that Mario Puzo is credited
with writing the first two? That little fact probably explains
Marlon Brando's appearance in the role of Superman's father, Jor-El. And while Brando has recently concerned
himself more with the "wily Filipino" than with his own
acting career, the once-great actor has fared slightly better
than *Superman III*'s three stars: Christopher Reeve, who is
confined to a wheelchair; Richard Pryor, who has been af-
flicted with a debilitating disease; and Margot Kidder, who
cuts a fine cloth of a woman ... in a straitjacket. Here are
five lines from some super hero movies.

1. "Prince Barin, I'm not your enemy—Ming is."
2. "How am I supposed to get a Pulitzer Prize writing stories about a pink bear?"
3. "Where does he get those wonderful toys?"
4. "I don't want to go to jail because there are robbers and rapers and rapers who rape robbers."
5. "I'm considering nothing less than world domination."

1. **Flash Gordon** (Sam J. Jones) in *Flash Gordon*
2. **Lois Lane** (Margot Kidder) in *Superman II*
3. **Jack Napier/The Joker** (Jack Nicholson) in *Batman*
4. **Gus Gorman** (Richard Pryor) in *Superman III*
5. **Selena** (Faye Dunaway) in *Supergirl*

Deities of the '80s—Michael Keaton

Any guy who plays Johnny Dangerously, Mr. Mom, Betelguese, and Batman has to have some serious mojo working for him. Born Michael Douglas (you see why he changed his name, don't you?), Keaton got his start in television playing a member of the Flying Zucchini Brothers on an early '70s episode of *Mr. Rogers' Neighborhood*. In 1982 he landed his first movie role, playing a pimp with Henry Winkler in *Night Shift*. (If you look closely, you can see Kevin Costner playing a "frat boy" in one of his earliest, most challenging roles.) This was Keaton's ticket to stardom, and he spent the rest of the decade cashing in. Now, in the '90s, when he's not making horrible Christmas movies (*Jack Frost*, eek!), he sits on the advisory board of the Pittsburgh Penguins, where he's been known to replace scouting videotapes with copies of the *Mighty Ducks* movies.

1. "I'm an escaped mental patient with a history of violence."
2. "I want you to do me a favor. I want you to tell all your friends about me."
3. "I'm the ghost with the most, babe."
4. "Thank you, and thanks for my chip. And thanks for not smoking."
5. "Look, here's the deal: Two years ago the underwear factory closed down in Hadleyville, right?"
6. "You got those. I like those on a woman."
7. "Irv, we were never *in* aisle seven."
8. "Is this a great country or what?"

1. **Billy** in *The Dream Team*
2. **Batman/Bruce Wayne** in *Batman*
3. **Betelgeuse** in *Beetlejuice*
4. **Daryl Poynter** in *Clean and Sober*
5. **Hunt Stevenson** in *Gung Ho*
6. **Johnny Kelly** in *Johnny Dangerously*
7. **Jack Butler** in *Mr. Mom*
8. **Bill Blazejowski** in *Night Shift*

"I am your father, Luke. Come to the
dark side, you hoser."

Take off, eh!

Beer, belches, vomit, hockey, *Star Wars* references, and a theme song performed by Rush: What self-respecting male wouldn't love ***Strange Brew***? Loosely based on *Hamlet* (if you can believe that), the movie tells the tale of Canadian brothers Bob and **Doug** McKenzie (Rick Moranis and Dave Thomas), who land jobs at the Elsinore brewery after trying to convince the manufacturer that they found a dead mouse in one of their beers. From there, the two "knobs" get roped into a dispute with the owner and discover that Brewmeister Smith (Max von Sydow) is about to take over the world with mind-controlling beer. Beauty, eh?

All Mixed Up, Part V

1. "I am so bad I should be in detention."
2. "He's got more humor in his little pinky than you have in your whole pinky."
3. "How could something so small create so much of something so disgusting?"
4. "You watch him. I shot someone. I have to leave the country."
5. "There's nothing wrong with going nowhere, son. It's a privilege of youth."
6. "We're now a quarter of an inch tall, and sixty-four feet from the house."
7. "There's nothing more boring than people who love you."
8. "See you at the finish line—wherever that may be."
9. "It's the only time when a black man can wave a stick at a white man and not start a riot."
10. "I've seen the future. It's a bald-headed man from New York."
11. "Mon crayon est large."
12. "Every time I call you're either taking a bath, washing your hair, or you're out of the country."
13. "I'm gonna kill the bitch. You want something?"
14. "This menstruation thing? It's a scam. Women are so lucky."
15. "We got el shafto grande—we got no place to stay."
16. "Why did you say 'I do' with me when you're still saying 'I did' to him?"

1. **Julio** (Taylor Negron) in *Easy Money*

2. **Sally** (Fran Drescher) in *The Hollywood Knights*

3. **Michael Kellam** (Steve Guttenberg) in *Three Men and a Baby*

4. **Larry** (Tom Hulce) in *Parenthood*

5. **Gardner Barnes** (Kevin Costner) in *Fandango*

6. **Nick Szalinski** (Robert Oliveri) in *Honey, I Shrunk the Kids*

7. **Barry** (Eric Bogosian) in *Talk Radio*

8. **Leon** (Alan Solomon) in *Midnight Madness*

9. **Anderson** (Gene Hackman) in *Mississippi Burning*

10. **David Howard** (Albert Brooks) in *Lost in America*

11. **Jonathan** (Anthony Edwards) in *Gotcha!*

12. **Ronald Miller** (Patrick Dempsey) in *Can't Buy Me Love*

13. **Larry** (Billy Crystal) in *Throw Momma from the Train*

14. **Dave Frasier** (Gary Riley) in *Summer School*

15. **Stu** (Paul Land) in *Spring Break*

16. **Ira** (Charles Grodin) in *Seems Like Old Times*

"If you'd like me to provide you with some vital statistics that can't be measured in a public place, I'd be happy to do so."

Little Miss Muffet
Sat on her tuffet
Along with Andrew Dice Clay
Along came a writer
Who crept up beside her
And said,
"Nice $%#*@*! career, you jerkoff."
OHHHH!

Yes, this conceit of turning a nursery rhyme into a cheap vulgar joke made the Dice Man famous for about ten seconds in the late '80s when his stand-up routine catapulted him to stardom. Clay started his acting career playing a chunkhead in '80s classics *Private Resort* (which was a *Spring Break* rip-off), *Night Patrol* (which stars dwarf extraordinaire Billy Barty), and this one, ***Casual Sex?***, where he basically plays himself in the guise of a character named **Vinny**. In 1990, Clay got his shot at superstardom, landing the leading role in the rock-and-roll comedy/crime story *The Adventures of Ford Fairlane*. Clearly, he blew his chance, because these days all Clay seems to do is get into shouting matches with Jackie "the Joke Man" Martling (an equally unfunny stand-up comic) on *The Howard Stern Show*.

I Ain't the Worst That You've Seen

Actually, the movies in this section *are* the worst that we've seen. And though most of the worst movies of the '80s were incredibly bad sequels (see *Caddyshack II* and *Jaws 3-D* in our section on bad sequels, p. 207), not all of them were. Here are a few lines from our most hated films of the decade, and yes, the abominable buddy film *Collision Course* (starring Pat Morita and Jay Leno!) is one of them. But please don't take offense if one of your favorite movies of all time made this list or if you're related to one of the directors. Remember, film is a very subjective medium, and one man's *Yor, the Hunter from the Future* is another man's *Raging Bull*. Something like that.

1. "But I'm not the number one agent. I retired seven years ago."
2. "We did not fire on two Americans in the desert."
3. "Every duck has his limit, and you scum have pushed me over the line."
4. "Now, in this proletarian stew which we laughingly call society, these attributes are not always advantageous."
5. "I trust God will understand. I'm not so sure about the neighbors."
6. "I shall invent an entirely new torture, against which there is no possible defense."
7. "Ah-ah. Bust my ass no good."
8. "Lucky for me this room is soundproof. That way nobody gets to hear me beating the truth out of you."

1. **Leonard Parker** (Bill Cosby) in *Leonard Part 6*
2. **Jim Harrison** (Charles Grodin) in *Ishtar*
3. **Howard T. Duck** (Tim Rose) in *Howard the Duck*[*]
4. **Douglas Benoit** (John Hurt) in *From the Hip*
5. **Yentl** (Barbra Streisand) in *Yentl*
6. **Fu Manchu** (Peter Sellers) in *The Fiendish Plot of Dr. Fu Manchu*
7. **Fujitsuka Natsuo** (Pat Morita) in *Collision Course*
8. **Gabriel Cash** (Kurt Russell) in *Tango & Cash*

[*]Actually, George Lucas favorite Tim Rose is just one of eight people listed in the credits as "Howard T. Duck."

"You know what a love letter is? It's a bullet from a f**king gun."

We know this is supposed to be a family book, but it's impossible to quote **Frank Booth** (Dennis Hopper) in *Blue Velvet* without using the *f*-word—our apologies to librarians across America who have already ordered several copies of this book for their K-through-6 sections. Anyway, *Blue Velvet,* written and directed by David Lynch, portrays a small community with the oddest assortment of weirdos since Tod Browning's *Freaks*. In fact, Hopper (who's not so stable to begin with) plays the wheezing sociopath Booth, who just might be the sickest, most twisted character to ever grace the big screen. And Dean Stockwell's rendition of Roy Orbison's "In Dreams" is enough to make you go out and rent *The Elephant Man* just for a dose of normalcy.

Deities of the '80s—Dennis Quaid

Don't worry, we're just as surprised as you are that Dennis Quaid (who is now married to Meg Ryan, the lucky bastard) is a deity of the '80s. But believe it or not, Randy's infinitely more handsome younger brother was quite the busy thespian throughout the decade. For God's sake, the man played a grown-up Mike Brody in *Jaws 3-D*. If that doesn't get your attention, we're not sure what will. It kind of makes you wish that cute little Mike Brody had been devoured by the great white in the first movie, doesn't it? But nonetheless, Quaid was pretty prolific—he was even in a movie called *G.O.R.P.* (not *Garp*), whatever that is—so we decided to give him praise the only way we know how. Of course, if you disagree, you can send a letter to International Creative Management out in Los Angeles. I'm sure they'd be thrilled that someone is even remotely interested in discussing the acting merits of their client.

1. "Well, if I'm going to hell, I'm going there playing the piano."
2. "When things are at their darkest, pal, it's a brave man that can kick back and party."
3. "This is New Orleans, darlin'. Folks have a certain way of doing things down here."
4. "All right. If he did it, I'm gonna vote guilty. If he's innocent, I don't want that on my conscience."
5. "If one receives evil from another, let one not do evil in return."
6. "Who was the best pilot I ever saw? Well, you're looking at him."

1. **Jerry Lee Lewis** in *Great Balls of Fire!*
2. **Lieutenant Tuck Pendelton** in *Innerspace*
3. **Remy McSwain** in *The Big Easy*
4. **Eddie Sanger** in *Suspect*
5. **Davidge** in *Enemy Mine*
6. **Gordon Cooper** in *The Right Stuff*

"All right, good news first. Roberta's not working with the greaseball."

Here's an '80s pop-culture dilemma for you. For the rest of your life you must do one of the following: listen to Patrick Swayze sing or watch Madonna act. Can you imagine a lifetime waking up in the morning to Swayze's synthed-up, overwrought "She's Like the Wind"? Or how about never being able to read the paper without *Who's That Girl?* or *Shanghai Surprise* playing on your TV in the background?

Ultimately, though, you'd have to choose watching Madonna act, because for at least two hours a day you'd get to watch her as **Susan** in 1985's ***Desperately Seeking Susan***. It's not a great movie, but it has one of the hippest supporting casts you'll ever find, including brilliant '80s stand-up comic Steven Wright, legendary punk rocker Richard Hell, and Indie film all-stars Rockets Redglare, Richard Edson, John Lurie, Giancarlo Esposito, and John Turturro.

"I'll be taking these Huggies, and, uh, whatever cash you got."

If you're the nephew of Francis Ford Coppola, there's a good chance you'll land a part in a movie at some point in your life. Nicolas Cage (né Coppola) was able to turn a bunch of offbeat roles in the '80s into an Oscar in the '90s. ***Raising Arizona*** was the break-out movie for both Cage (who played the confused **H. I. McDonnough**) and the Coen brothers (Ethan and Joel), who wrote and directed this quirky 1987 comedy.

Deities of the '80s—John Cusack

John Cusack—our superhero of '80s movies. First off, he appeared in an array of great films from cult hits like *Better Off Dead* and *Tapeheads* to more mainstream successes like *Sixteen Candles* and *Say Anything*. . . . But our real appreciation of Cusack has nothing to do with his classic '80s movies. It was the cool retro soundtrack of 1997's *Grosse Pointe Blank* that helped jump-start this mint '80s revival and got us a book contract in the first place. Go John!

Actually, early in John's career, his older sister Joan paved the way for his entry into show business. But it didn't take long for John to step out of her shadow. After all, *his* minor character in *Sixteen Candles* has a name, Bryce, while Joan's character is just credited as "Girl Wearing a Scoliosis Brace."

1. "Joe, she's written sixty-five songs. Sixty-five! They're all about you, and they're all about pain."
2. "I want to put it on the record somewheres that I asked for a separate trial and was refused."
3. "You look ravishing and I'd like to chew on your thighs."
4. "If we give in to these people, we're giving in to all the cute and fuzzy bunnies in the world."
5. "Hey, don't start with me, porcupine. Come here, come here, give me a hug."
6. "Gee, I'm real sorry your mom blew up, Ricky."
7. "What the hell's wrong with being stupid once in a while?"
8. "You know, black and white would just capture the moment so nicely, wouldn't it?"

1. **Lloyd Dobler** in *Say Anything . . .*
2. **Buck Weaver** in *Eight Men Out*
3. **Ivan Alexeev** in *Tapeheads*
4. **Hoops McCann** in *One Crazy Summer*
5. **Denny Lachance** in *Stand by Me*
6. **Lane Myer** in *Better Off Dead*
7. **Walter "Gib" Gibson** in *The Sure Thing*
8. **Bryce** in *Sixteen Candles*

"Six weeks! I can't do six weeks!"

We chose this line to be the last line of *Say Anything* for several reasons—not the least of which is to reference the amount of time we had to write this book. But we also chose this line because it's from another one of our favorite '80s movies—Martin Scorsese's incredibly underrated **The King of Comedy**. This line is from the fantasy sequence in which **Rupert Pupkin** (Robert De Niro) is going on to Jerry Langford (Jerry Lewis) about how difficult it would be to appear as the replacement host on *The Jerry Langford Show*. Lewis is amazing in this movie. Probably because in the role of the hyperfamous, bitter, sleazy TV star, he didn't have to act (sorry, Francophiles). The best quote from the film is one that sort of sums it all up for us: "Better to be king for a night than a schmuck for a lifetime."